Cambridge Elements

Elements in Second Language Acquisition
edited by
Alessandro Benati
The University of Hong Kong
John W. Schwieter
Wilfrid Laurier University, Ontario

THE ACQUISITION OF ASPECT IN A SECOND LANGUAGE

Stefano Rastelli
University of Pavia

CAMBRIDGE
UNIVERSITY PRESS

University Printing House, Cambridge CB2 8BS, United Kingdom

One Liberty Plaza, 20th Floor, New York, NY 10006, USA

477 Williamstown Road, Port Melbourne, VIC 3207, Australia

314–321, 3rd Floor, Plot 3, Splendor Forum, Jasola District Centre, New Delhi – 110025, India

79 Anson Road, #06–04/06, Singapore 079906

Cambridge University Press is part of the University of Cambridge.

It furthers the University's mission by disseminating knowledge in the pursuit of education, learning, and research at the highest international levels of excellence.

www.cambridge.org
Information on this title: www.cambridge.org/9781108829038
DOI: 10.1017/9781108903455

First published 2020

A catalogue record for this publication is available from the British Library.

ISBN 978-1-108-82903-8 Paperback
ISSN 2517-7974 (online)
ISSN 2517-7966 (print)

The Acquisition of Aspect in a Second Language

Elements in Second Language Acquisition

DOI: 10.1017/9781108903455
First published online:November 2020

Stefano Rastelli
University of Pavia

Author for correspondence: Stefano Rastelli, stefano.rastelli@unipv.it

Abstract: The acquisition of Aspect is a central area in Second Language Acquisition research, and the subject of hundreds of papers and dozens of edited volumes, monographies and special issues. This Element provides the reader not only with a concise and plain presentation of the main hypotheses advanced in the past, but also with an overview of contemporary research. The comparison of behavioral (production–comprehension), processing and statistical data is improving – and partially changing – our understanding of how learners acquire the aspectual distinctions of the target language.

Keywords: aspect, second language acquisition, lexical aspect hypothesis

ISBNs: 9781108829038 (PB), 9781108903455 (OC)
ISSNs: 2517-7974 (online), 2517-7966 (print)

Contents

1 What Are the Key Concepts?

1.1 Aspect: A Basic Definition

Aspect is a multifaceted property of predicates – with syntactic, semantic and pragmatic correlates – which is shared by many languages. This Element concerns whether and how this property is learned by *second* language (L2) learners. This section introduces key concepts and basic definitions. Let us consider the following English sentence:

(1) *When Marco looked through the window, he saw Elena watching TV*

In this sentence there are three different English predicates indicating the event of perceiving something with sight: *looked through the window, saw Elena, watching TV.* Unlike native speakers of English, L2 learners may find it difficult to choose among the verbs *look, see* and *watch* occurring in those predicates.[1] In order to understand why, one needs to reflect on the amount of information that a native English speaker masters when representing the events corresponding to those three predicates. Likely, they will imagine the event 'looked through the window' as intentional – that is, performed by an animate subject who must decide to look through the window before doing it. In contrast, the event 'he saw Elena' may be regarded as unintentional, with the object entering the visual field unexpectedly (i.e., Marco could not necessarily predict what he was going to see through the window). Moreover, whereas the event expressed by the predicate 'he saw Elena' is instantaneous (i.e., the vision of 'Elena watching TV' formed on Marco's retina in a few milliseconds), the event of Elena 'watching TV' is prolonged. Finally, while the event 'he saw' culminates (i.e., it comes to an end once Marco's eyes perceive Elena), the events 'Elena was watching TV' and 'Marco looked through the window' have no culmination since there is no natural endpoint in their meaning – that is, there is nothing that prevents such events from being prolonged endlessly. These examples show that also very similar predicates such as *look through the window, see Elena* and *watch TV* can be made of very different 'fabric'. This fabric is their internal makeup: how the event described by a given predicate unfolds in time, how this temporal texture may change depending on the object and on the subject performing the action, and how the predicate fits real-world situations. Bearing this in mind, and following a well-established tradition, we will refer to the *internal makeup* of

[1] Following a long-established tradition, in this Element I will use the term 'verb' to refer to the lexical entry (both the lemma and the lexeme). I will reserve the term 'predicate' for the verb phrase (VP) that comprises the verb and its obligatory arguments.

predicates as 'lexical Aspect' (LAsp) (Section 1.4).[2] In this Element, we adhere to the view that LAsp – in spite of its name – is not just 'lexical'. In fact LAsp does not pertain only to the lexical entry (the verb in isolation), but to at least three factors: syntax (the kind of verb arguments and adjuncts at the verb phrase [VP] level), semantics (including theta-roles and macro-roles hierarchy) and pragmatics (a speaker's knowledge of how the event designed by that predicate may and may not occur in the world). There are striking similarities – and important differences – in how speakers of different languages can conceive the LAsp of events described by seemingly equivalent predicates. This fact suggests caution in the crosslinguistic comparison of LAsp and supports the view that the law of physics (laws of nature), ontology (how the mind conceives the events) and language (how such events are encoded and how they can be presented in a sentence) are entwined but separate levels of representation (Section 1.8).

Besides LAsp, the term 'Aspect' captures another supposedly universal property of predicates. In the English sentence (1), the different verb morphemes (*-ed* in 'looked' and *-ing* in 'watching') automatically signal that the hearer/reader should mentally project the events in two different scenarios. The morpheme *–ed* of 'looked' frames the event from the perspective of its final boundary. When encountering this morpheme, the hearer/reader instinctively zooms out and marks the limits of 'looking through the window' because they know that the event is completed.

The term 'completed' needs an explanation. It should be confounded neither with 'past' (Section 1.3) nor with 'finished'. As we will see (Section 1.5), 'completed' (and the corresponding substantive 'completion') means that there has been enough of 'looking through the window' in order for the story to progress to the next stage (in our case, to the event of Marco 'seeing Elena'). In other words, the hearer/reader can disregard whether the event of looking through the window is finished or not, as it is no longer interesting for the meaning of the sentence (or for the story). What counts is that the event has come to a completion – that is, there has been 'enough of it' in order for a hearer/reader to move on.

Unlike the morpheme *–ed*, the morpheme *–ing* does not mark the limits of the event. When encountering *–ing*, the hearer/reader zooms in and thinks of the event 'Elena watching TV' as ongoing. When processing 'watching TV', the hearer/reader knows two things: (a) Elena likely started watching TV before Marco saw her, and (b) Elena may or may not continue watching TV after Marco

[2] In order to avoid the assumption that LAsp concerns only the verb, many authors prefer the term 'inherent aspect'.

sees her. To say it differently, while the events 'looked through the window' and 'saw her' are presented from the outside, the event 'Elena watching TV' is presented from the inside, regardless of its boundaries (its beginning and its end). In English – but also in Spanish, French, Italian and many other languages – speakers use verb morphology to zoom in or out and – in general – to impose a certain perspective on the events. The whole set of grammatical and lexical means through which a speaker presents an event as bounded or ongoing is called 'grammatical Aspect' (GA; Section 1.5).

(Un)boundedness is not the only perspective that the speaker may decide to adopt in order to present an event. Moreover, there are other means to express GA besides verb morphology. For example, adverbs and adverbial expressions such as 'always' and 'every day' can be used within the VP to underline that the event is continuous ('Marco was always looking through the window') or habitual ('Marco would look through the window every day'). Different languages utilize different means (lexical, syntactic, derivational) to express GA. The adjective 'grammatical' in the expression GA is not meant to restrict our field of inquiry to the Standard Average European languages, but it refers to the fact that – in the most-studied second languages – the perspective on the event is usually marked by means of overt grammatical morphemes.

1.2 The Term 'Aspect': A Clarification

Research on L1 and L2 Aspect is indebted to Slavic and Germanic linguists of the last century, who introduced a crucial distinction between 'Aspect' and '*Aktionsart*'. This distinction was subsequently – and sometimes improperly – extended to other languages, thus paving the way for the contemporary study of Aspect. These linguists were the first to acknowledge that the internal fabric or predicate makeup (which we have called LAsp) and the speaker's perspective on the event (what we have called GA) were separate but tightly entwined linguistic categories. By analyzing the structure of Slavic languages, these linguists noticed that many different affixes can combine systematically with the verb root to give rise to many semantic and aspectual combinations. Some such affixes clearly serve to bind the event designed by the predicate, whereas others present the event as unbounded and ongoing. Importantly, some affixes change the way the event is viewed but not the meaning of the verb. For example, in Polish *kupić* means 'to have bought' whereas *kupować* means 'to be buying'. On the other hand, in Slavic languages there also exist other affixes that change both the perspective on the event and the meaning of the root predicate. For example, in Polish the predicate *grales* means 'you were playing/played', whereas *wygrales* means 'you won/win'. In this case, the prefix *wy-* also shifts the meaning of the verb from one phase of the event to another – that is, from the process (playing) to one of its possible outcomes (winning).

As a consequence of the rich, articulated and intricate suffix–prefix structured alternations in Slavic languages, in the early decades of the last century some proposed that the term 'Aspect' should be reserved exclusively for the binary opposition between bounded (perfective) and unbounded (imperfective), as conveyed by inflectional morphemes (see Borik et al., 2003; for a historical review, see also Mlynarczyk, 2004, chapter 2). The term 'Aspect' is a calque after the Russian *vid* '(a) view' and comes from the Latin *aspectus*, the past participle of the verb *aspiciere* 'to look at'. In contrast, it was proposed that the German term 'Aktionsart' (literally 'manner of action') should be used only to denote the category that captures regularities in the semantics of aspectual affixes. In this vein, Comrie (1976, p. 7) wrote that the term 'Aspect' refers to the *grammaticalization* of a semantic aspectual distinction, while the term 'Aktionsart' refers to the *lexicalization* of a semantic aspectual distinction by means of derivational morphology. The situation gets more intricate if one considers, as we have seen, that even some fully 'grammaticalized' aspectual affixes in Slavic languages may or may not also have an idiosyncratic lexical meaning. For example, in Bulgarian some perfective prefixes just encode the completion of the event (*pis* 'write' > *na-piša* 'write in full'), whereas others also change the meaning of the verb (*pre-piša* 'write again, copy') (Slabakova, 2001, p. 83).

To sum up, modern linguists tried to extend the 'Aspect vs. Aktionsart' dichotomy, which was originally meant to account for the different functions of the many aspectual affixes of Slavic languages, to GA and LAsp in languages that do not have aspectual affixes. Since the situation of Slavic languages is not comparable to that of, say, English or Spanish, some stated that Slavic languages and the terminology that describes them cannot provide the ideal prototype for describing any non-Slavic aspectual system (e.g., Bertinetto & Delfitto, 2000, p. 189). Although the debate is not yet over, many linguists continue to utilize a technical terminology that fits the morphological richness of Slavic languages, but that hardly constitutes a benchmark for aspectual description across languages or a tool to explain L2 acquisition. To avoid this danger, in this Element we will give up the term 'Aktionsart' and will instead use 'Aspect' in its broader sense (as encompassing both LAsp and GA), as will be made clearer in Sections 1.4 and 1.5. It should be also kept in mind that although most examples in this Element come from languages where LAsp is encoded lexically and GA is encoded morphologically, this situation by no means represents the prevailing norm in the majority of world languages.

1.3 Aspect and Tense

The linguistic category of Aspect must be distinguished from the linguistic category of Tense. Tense "locate[s] situations either at the same time as the present moment . . . or prior to the present moment, or subsequent to the present moment" (Comrie, 1985, p. 14). This means that Tense grammaticalizes a temporal location in an absolute way by placing events on a timeline (Comrie, 1985, pp. 9–13), regardless of how the event is presented or flows in time. Importantly, the timeline on which the event is placed is purely linguistic: 'present', 'past' and 'future' make sense only in a given utterance or act of speech. In other words, the location in time that Tense provides is meaningful only with respect to the time at which the speaker produces an utterance and/or with reference to a point in time that has been specified in the sentence (e.g., by means of adverbs such as 'before', 'already', etc.). In contrast, the linguistic category of Aspect pertains to "viewing the internal temporal constituency of a situation" (Comrie, 1976, p. 3) and characterizes how a speaker views its 'temporal contour'. In sum, while Tense locates an event in time, Aspect frames the event from the speaker's perspective and describes how it flows in time.

1.4 Lexical Aspect (LAsp)

We have said that LAsp is the internal makeup or the 'fabric' of predicates. In her influential 1991 study, Smith writes that aspectual systems provide a choice of 'situation type' and 'viewpoint'. Situation type pertains to LAsp; viewpoint pertains to GA. Situation types are categorized in terms of the temporal structure of situations – that is, the beginning, the end and the duration of an event or a state (Smith, 1991, p. 3). For this reason, Smith calls LAsp 'situation Aspect'. We have seen that LAsp refers to how the events designed by predicates in a given language unfold in time: if they have a duration ('walk in the park') or are instantaneous ('sneeze'); if they culminate ('die') or are monotonic ('work'); if they express a change of state ('bloom') or a permanent quality of an entity ('being tall'). As the *temporal texture* of a predicate, LAsp is independent of temporal location (whether the corresponding event occurred in the past, present or future: see Section 1.3) but is strongly dependent on the nature of internal and external predicate arguments, and also partly on a speaker's knowledge of how the events described by that predicate may or may not occur in the real world (Section 1.10).

1.4.1 Aspectual Classes

According to Filip (2011), in the 1970s – also under the influence of formal and generative approaches to semantics – LAsp and the study of Slavic morphology (affixes) parted ways definitively, the latter being associated stably with lexical semantics. However, the tradition of dividing predicates into aspectual classes based on their intrinsic meaning is older. Indeed, the most enduring distinctions were introduced between 1940 and 1960. During that period, scholars tried to individuate the common building blocks of LAsp across languages. Among the protagonists of this line of research were Ryle (1949), Vendler (1957), Kenny (1963) and Dowty (1979). Ryle (1949) was the first to contrast 'achievements' (end-oriented) with 'activities' that lack any end (Ryle, 1949, p. 150), whereas Kenny (1963) set up the distinction between 'activities' and 'states'. But the most influential author is without a doubt Zeno Vendler.

Vendler (1967, pp. 99–101) wrote that different verbs presuppose or entail different 'time schemata', some of which admit discontinuity ('run') and some of which don't ('believe'); some of which are homogeneous ('push a cart') and some with a logical and necessary endpoint ('reach the top'); some lasting for a certain interval ('swim') and some without any duration at all. Vendler classified English verbs at least in their dominant use according to four categories for which he significantly introduces the word 'term' (e.g., 'accomplishment terms') rather than 'verb' (1967, p. 107). Such classes or terms were intended to capture "the most common time schemata implied by the use of English verbs" (Vendler,1957, p. 144). According to Vendler, the four aspectual classes were as follows:

STATES:	desire, want, love, hate, dominate;
ACTIVITIES:	run, walk, swim, push (a cart);
ACHIEVEMENTS:	recognize, reach, find, win (the race), start/stop/resume, be born/die;
ACCOMPLISHMENTS:	run a mile, paint a picture, grow up, recover from illness.

After Vender's quadripartition, accomplishment and achievement terms were named 'telic' and activities and states were named 'atelic'. According to Garey (1957, p. 106), who introduced this terminology after the Greek noun *telos* (end), "telic verbs are verbs expressing an action tending towards a goal" while "atelic verbs . . . are verbs which do not involve any goal nor endpoint in their semantic structure, but denote actions that are realized as soon as they begin." Filip (2011, p. 1189) sums up the rationale behind the Vendlerian subdivision as follows: Both accomplishments and activities involve periods of time, but only accomplishments also require that they be unique and definite (Vendler, 1967, p. 149). Both states and achievements involve time instants, but only achievements "occur at a single moment" (p. 147), while states hold at any instant during the interval at which they are true (p. 149). The idea that only activities and accomplishments 'go on in time' is taken to motivate their compatibility with the 'continuous Tense' – that is, the progressive, a property not shared by states and achievements.

Many authors noticed that most lexical entries that Vendler quoted as examples of accomplishment terms were not lexical verbs but actual VPs: for example, 'paint a picture', 'build a chair', 'build a house', 'write a tale', 'read a tale', 'attend class', 'play chess'. All these expressions have an object which contributes to their meaning. In the syntactic account of Aspect described in Section 2.4, VPs are never made by verbs alone, but by the verb in conjunction with its (obligatory) arguments.[3] Verkuyl (2015, p. 24) – referring to Vendler – observed that "it is simply wrong linguistically speaking to call verb phrases like 'win the race' and 'discover a treasure' a verb." In fact, examples of how the same verb changes aspectual category depending on the argument abound even in Vendler's work. For instance, 'believe in the stork' (vs. 'believe you') and 'reach the top' (vs. 'reach a readership') are classified as stative and achievement, respectively, because of their object NPs. Also, the verb 'think' may have two opposite actional readings depending on sentence completion: 'she's thinking of Tom' is stative vs. 'she thinks that Tom is stupid' is achievement.

Reflecting on these and other examples, one should consider whether Vendler was really thinking of verbs alone or rather of something else (syntax and argument structures). As Verkuyl (2005, p. 24) noted, Dowty (1979, 1991) was the first to use the Vendlerian aspectual classes to identify and characterize the lexical differences between verbs at the level of lexical entries. Dowty's work in fact represented a fundamental step toward a lexicalist interpretation of Vendler, and of LAsp in general. According to Dowty, each verb is attributed a *kernel meaning* with its own, well-defined lexical-semantic representation composed of three semantic primitives or aspectual connectives (CAUSE, BECOME and DO). Such connectives operate on stative predicate representation, which is assumed to underlie every predicate. When a predicate happens to enter two or more aspectual classes, then a derivational pattern is introduced to permit an appropriate 'aspectual shift'. To give one example taken from van Valin (1990), in sentence (3) an adaptation of V's aspectual-semantic representation is obtained by the introduction of a rule ↑ [+delimited quantity] operating on the kernel meaning of 'eat' in (2):

(2) *John ate spaghetti* (activity)
(3) *John ate the spaghetti* (accomplishment)

[3] The distinction between arguments and adjuncts, which is widely disputed, falls beyond the purpose of this book.

Dowty's lexical decomposition of predicates and his lexicalist interpretation of Vendler were carried on by Foley and van Valin (1984) and van Valin (1990, 2005). They attributed to each verb argument a gradient of semantic roles which maps with its lexical-semantic representation. This machinery allowed the authors to introduce a split in the set of stative verbs that was added between, for instance, agentive statives, nonagentive statives, interval statives, be statives and possibly statives. The same operation was carried out with accomplishment verbs (single-change predicates and complex-change predicates). Here are a few examples of how the different combinations of aspectual connectives (CAUSE, BECOME and DO) can account for shifts of aspectual classes of the same verb:

STATES:	*the watch is broken*: BE (watch, [broken])
ACHIEVEMENTS:	*The watch broke*: BECOME broken (watch)
ACTIVITIES:	*Susan ran*: run (Susan)
ACCOMPLISHMENT:	*Susan ran to the house*: [run(Susan)]
CAUSE	[BECOME BE-at (house, Susan)]

These examples show how a single verb such as 'break' can enter multiple aspectual classes depending on the aspectual connectives.

1.4.2 The Telic–Atelic Distinction

The most widespread conceptual opposition among LAsp categories is that between telic and atelic predicates. Telic predicates have a virtual resulting state, or 'culmination point'. When thinking of events described by telic predicates, such as 'paint a wall' or 'build a house', speakers can imagine the culmination point – that is, the wall being completely painted or the house being completely built. This culmination point is virtual because the sentence may or may not describe it explicitly. For example, in English, the event 'paint the wall' can be described with perfective morphology (e.g., 'today they painted the wall in one hour') or with imperfective-progressive morphology (e.g., 'today they are painting the wall'). Atelic predicates, such as 'push a cart' or 'take a stroll', lack a virtual culmination point.

The culmination point is sometimes seen as the head of a projection called 'event structure' (Pustejovsky, 1991). Both interval semantics[4] (Dowty, 1979) and the mereological approaches (Champollion & Krifka, 2016) – although

[4] Many sentences in many languages involve explicit references to interval of time rather than to instants of time. The proponents of interval semantics argue that the logical space that allows the correct interpretation of the truth-value of any proposition is defined by a couple formed by a possible world (W) and an uninterrupted interval of time (I) where the proposition holds true.

from very different perspectives – differentiate between telic and atelic events by the presence or absence of a culmination point. For example, Krifka (1992) – partly following Vendler (1967) and Bennett and Partee (2004) – coupled a culmination point's presence with nonhomogeneous events and its absence with homogeneous ones. Homogeneity concerns how events flow in time. 'Pushing a chair' is homogeneous because it lacks any qualitatively different subinterval throughout its duration. By contrast, 'painting a wall' is not homogeneous because it involves a special subinterval: the moment when the wall is completely painted.

Dowty (1979) characterizes homogeneity such that, if φ is an activity that is true with respect to interval I, then φ is also true with respect to any sufficiently large subinterval of I. The interval and the subinterval are assumed to be homogeneous. Telic events violate this assumption because they have a richer, differentiated (nonhomogeneous) internal structure. Such structure is richer because it includes a result, which, according to Dowty (1979), is often linguistically encoded by a particular class of direct objects called 'incremental themes' (e.g., 'the wall'). Some aspectual diagnostics reveal predicates' subinterval property (the fact of having or not having a culmination point). For example, the question in sentence (4) is a test that distinguishes atelic ('Yes') from telic ('No') in noniterative, nonhabitual predicates:

(4) *If you stop in the middle of V-ing, have you V-ed?*

Because of the nonhomogeneity of their subintervals, telic predicates (achievements and accomplishments) elicit "No" answers to this question.

1.4.3 Problems with Classification of LAsp

Any classification of LAsp raises at least two problems. First and foremost are classification disagreements among scholars, both within and across languages. As an example of the first kind, Housen (2002, p. 166) classifies the English verb 'grow up' as atelic, despite Vendler (1967, p. 108) placing it among telic verbs. We could also classify the corresponding Italian verb *crescere* 'grow up' as a gradual completion verb (Bertinetto & Delfitto, 2000) and, as such, telic. As long as misalignment between parameters of different analyses is not clearly recognized and adequately handled, noncomparability among classification outcomes will remain.

The second problem is the intrinsically elusive character of LAsp. LAsp categories are highly elusive because the judgment on the belonging of a verb to one class or another is far from clear cut, even for native speakers. Sometimes LAsp classification seems to be a matter of induction rather than deduction.

Lenci and Zarcone (2009) offer a 'stochastic' (based on probability) model of LAsp in order to underline its high variability and its strong dependence on the context. As far as L1 Italian is concerned, the aspectual shift (or 'Actional Hybridism', as it is called in Bertinetto, 1986) seems to be the norm rather than the exception. Lenci and Zarcone (2009) hypothesized that the interpretation of the LAsp value of a verb in context was the result of a complex integration of hybrid linguistic constraints which act as probabilistic soft constraints. Looking at performance data in written and spoken corpora, one is easily driven to believe that, under the appropriate conditions, almost every Italian verb may belong to two, and sometimes three and even four, different actional classes. For instance, among 3,429 verbal tokens of 33 V types extracted from the TreSSI corpus, the cases of univocal or almost univocal actional assignment (like the verb *vincere* 'win') are about 25 percent – that is, the great minority. On the other hand, the most frequent verbs – such as *fare* 'do/make', *andare* 'go', *dire* 'say', *dare* 'give' – can belong to at least three different aspectual categories depending on the context. Given this situation, one may wonder whether speaking of 'aspectual class' makes any sense. This concept is undoubtedly a useful one, provided that it is conceived in a gradient-like manner rather than in absolute terms.

1.4.4 Are LAsp Categories Universal?

When representing the LAsp of predicates, one may think of (a) an ideal, abstract 'corresponding event' and how such an event would unfold in the real world, regardless of the language describing it; (b) the prepositional content conveyed by the predicate and by the sentence (regardless of how the event unfolds); or (c) how a given language promotes particular aspects of reality and demotes others. Position (a) focuses on human cognition and on the laws of nature, disregarding crosslinguistic differences. Position (b) focuses on the language and disregards ontological considerations of reality. Position (c) adopts the perspective of linguistic relativity and privileges crosslinguistic comparison.

The three positions represent the pendulum swing of aspectual studies between linguistics and philosophy of the last 70 years at least. Some scholars tend to consider LAsp to be relatively similar across languages (e.g., Li &, Shirai, 2000, p. 4). For instance, Weist (2002, p. 36) maintains that 'the Vendler-like categories have broad crosslinguistic semantic and syntactic implications'. Smith (1991, xvi) wrote that the basic situation types appear generally, even if they vary from one language to another, because they 'are based in human cognitive abilities' (xvii). This does not mean that, for example, the equivalent to the English predicate 'understand' will display the same LAsp category in all languages. Yet, the English lemma 'understand' can indicate a state or an activity, depending on the object NP ('Marco understands everything' vs. 'Marco understands the joke'). Scholars in general acknowledge that LAsp categories are fuzzy and flexible both within and across languages, but some also insist that the predicates of the world languages share the same building blocks and that LAsp categories can in fact be considered semantic universals or 'cryptotypes' (a term created by linguist Benjamin Whorf). If this is true, the task for adult L2 learners would be just to recombine those building blocks, which are already present and working in the mind, and map them onto the novel L2 lexicon.

Other scholars (e.g., Tatevosov, 2002), claim that the Vendlerian classes are neither semantic primitives nor language universals, and that LAsp is at most a parameter (a bundle of features) that allows for different settings in different languages (Tatevosov, 2002, p. 324). Tatevosov (2002) quotes the following critical statement from Ebert (1995, p. 186): 'most often it is assumed that a verb or verb phrase has the same actional character as its closest English counterpart'. As we will see, the idea that LAsp categories are the mental ingredients of predicates in every language comes with many problems, including the risk of Anglo-centricity.

In this Element, we adopt the view that LAsp is a linguistic property of predicates. Native speakers cannot abstract away the LAsp of predicates from the peculiarities of all other elements occurring in the sentence. In the same way, L2 learners will have to reconstruct the LAsp categories of the L2 by putting together many different pieces of the aspectual puzzle (see Section 2). These pieces are GA, Syntax, Semantics, and even Pragmatics-Discourse (i.e., knowledge of the world). Dowty (1979, p. 185) stated that aspectual classification "is not a categorization of verbs, it is not a categorization of sentences, but rather of the propositions conveyed by utterances, given particular background assumptions by speaker and/or hearer about the nature of the situations under discussion". On the other hand, Verkuyl (2005, p. 27) specified that even the notion itself of culmination is ontological, not linguistic. According to Verkuyl, this notion is rooted in our tendency to give the final limit of any event a prominent place in the time course, but there is no detectable linguistic material at the VP level that specifically expresses a culmination point. This view highlights that aspectual classification should be seen as a purely linguistic operation, and labels such as 'stative', 'accomplishment', etc., make sense only in reference to the specific properties of predicates in a given language, not to the properties of the physical world ('the nature of the situation') or of the human mind. Michaelis (2004, p. 5) nicely sums up this idea by writing that aspectual categorization should be considered a product of the manner in which people, as producers and processors of texts, construe scenes, rather than as a reflection of the properties that situations have 'in the world'

1.4.5 Compositionality: A Bottom-up Approach to LAsp

The lexicalist approach to LAsp claims that a verb/predicate's aspectual class is determined and mediated by the lexical properties projected by the head V. This can be called the 'top-down' approach to LAsp. In this section, we present the alternative 'bottom-up' approach to LAsp proposed by Henk Verkuyl (1993). This author states that Vendler's quadripartition was ill founded because it ignores the basic principles of compositionality involved in building aspectual information. Verkuyl denies that aspectual classes are useful for the linguistic study of Tense and Aspect because Vendler's (and Dowty's) use of the term 'verb' is philosophical, not linguistic. Here 'philosophical' means that Vendler and Dowty – when assigning aspectual classes – did not look at how the VP is construed in a given language. Rather, they assumed the existence of a supposed kernel meaning of the verb, which in turn is derived by looking at how the corresponding event would occur in the world. For example, when Vendler assigned a *telos* (endpoint) to the predicate 'draw a circle', he reasoned 'downwards' by assuming that the noun 'circle' should force the kernel meaning of 'draw' (activity) toward a telic (accomplishment) interpretation. For this reason, Verkuyl suggests, Vendler calls 'draw a circle' simply a verb without questioning the specific ways in which 'draw' combines with 'circle' in that VP.

In the bottom-up, compositional approach to LAsp, all elements of the VP are not only connected (as in the top-down approach), they are also codetermined. According to the compositional approach, the verb 'draw' has no kernel meaning at all. Rather, it makes a constant contribution to the construal of any VP where it happens to occur, exactly as an atom contributes to any molecule it is a part of. The lexical entry 'draw' simply does not exist outside a VP. Any verb represents an atomic element of meaning which must always occur together with other atomic elements of meaning to form a bigger molecule (the VP). The rules by which the atoms combine to form molecules of aspectual meaning (the VPs) can be also highly language specific. Verkuyl (1999, p. 16) gives one famous example in which the atomic trait of meaning [±sqa] (specified quantity), carried by the English NPs 'a sandwich' (as opposed to 'sandwiches'), compositionally codetermines the terminative (telic) vs. the durative-iterative (atelic) character of the whole English VP in (5) and in (6):

(5) *Judith ate a sandwich* (telic)
(6) *Judith ate sandwiches* (atelic)

In these sentences, the lexical properties of the verb 'eat' – its kernel meaning – cannot be invoked in order to account for the aspectual shift between (5) and (6). It's not that the direct objects or internal arguments just contribute to LAsp by forcing the activity kernel meaning of 'eat' toward one interpretation or another. Rather, these atomic elements – together with the V – are the elements on which LAsp is built. This is because the verb 'eat' does not exist in isolation, as a pure monadic lexical entry, either in the language or in the mind. Said differently, when representing and processing the unit 'eat', one always thinks of who/what is eating whom/what.

Verkuyl's (1993, 1999, 2005) compositional approach to aspectual classification and to aspectual theory is designed for L1s, not for L2 learners' interlanguages. In spite of this, it can be relevant also for L2 acquisition. Let us anticipate here a more technical point which will be clearer in Section 2 of this book. Verkuyl's model accounts compositionally for the properties of V, which are here codetermined and derived bottom-up, starting from the combination of the semantic atomic property ±sqa (specified quantity) of the internal argument (NP2 in Figure 1) with the property ±addto (that expresses dynamic progress, change, nonstativity) of V. The complex semantic object at VP then combines (in a different and much more complicated way) with the external argument NP1, forming a tenseless sentence S which shows aspectual information labelled ±T (that expresses the features 'terminative' or 'durative'). Below this point is what Verkuyl calls 'Inner Aspect', while above this point is the domain of 'Outer Aspect', where the tenseless S comes into contact with principles (morphological features expressing Tense) in order to form the higher projection of S. I here adopt a simplified version of Verkuyl's theory especially because of his idea of unification of temporal and atemporal features (that are expressed, respectively, by the lower and the higher S in the same tree).

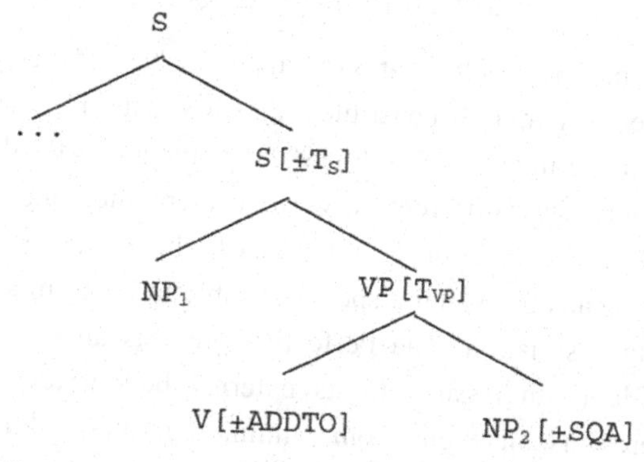

Figure 1 Verkuyl's scheme (Verkuyl, 2005, p. 20).

Verkuyl's theory is interesting for representing how L2 learners might acquire LAsp for a fundamental reason. If aspectual classes (which Verkuyl assumes to be state, process and event, following Comrie, 1976) are not conceived as properties of the V itself (Verkuyl, 2005, p. 23), then L2 learners are not expected to know in advance how many different meanings the same verb must have depending on the context. L2 learners should not memorize that 'eat' can be accomplishment or activity. Rather, they should look at the broader picture (the VP) and compute from scratch the LAsp of 'eat', depending on who is eating what. Therefore, when processing one among the following four versions of sentence (7a–d):

(7) a. *John discovered nothing* (state)
 b. *John discovered treasures* (activity)
 c. *John discovered three treasures* (accomplishment)
 d. *John discovered a treasure* (achievement)

L2 learners and also native speakers would always compute from scratch the meaning of the four different VPs ('discovered nothing' vs. 'discovered treasures', etc.) without necessarily assigning 'discover' a kernel meaning and an aspectual class in the target language. Absolute kernel meanings and aspectual classes probably do not even exist. As we will see in Section 2, especially L2 initial learners cannot be credited with the capacity for both labelling the aspectual class of L2 verbs and using complex coercion rules to shift LAsp classes where it is requested by the context. The LAsp of L2 predicates is perhaps more easily computed anew each time by putting together all the elements of a sentence than memorized once for all in the form of lexical entries (for a different application of Verkuy's theory to Second Language Acquisition [SLA], see González, 2013).

1.5 Grammatical Aspect

Comrie (1976, p. 16) wrote that GA distinguishes "different ways of viewing the internal temporal constituency of a situation". The expression 'viewpoint Aspect' utilized by Smith (1991) captures exactly this meaning. There are in fact many different ways to present the same situation in speech. We have noted (Section 1.1) that GA is the whole set of grammatical and lexical means by which a speaker is able to zoom in and zoom out when presenting a situation. The Perfective presents an event, so to say, from the outside (with regards to its external boundaries) whereas the Imperfective presents an event from within, regardless of its beginning and its end. Typological research (e.g., Dahl, 1985) evidenced that most languages in the world distinguish between perfective and imperfective Aspect and that the perfective/imperfective contrast is probably the typologically most prominent aspectual distinction (Bertinetto and Delfitto, 2000). In Romance languages, the perfective/imperfective contrast is confined to the past Tense, where Tense and Aspect are merged in morphology. For example, French opposes the Passé Simple *donna* 'gave.PERF' to the imparfait *donnait* 'gave. IMP'. Italian too opposes the passato remoto *donò* 'gave.PERF' to the imperfetto *donava* 'gaveIMP'. Not all languages fit the binary treatment seen for Romance languages. Some functions of the Perfective and of the Imperfective can be differently distributed across verb morphology, depending on the language. English, for example, has a progressive-imperfective form which only grammaticalizes the expression of ongoing events but not the habitual reading, whereas in Italian the progressive features both functions. Many authors have tried to characterize GA in terms of the speaker's perspective or 'viewpoint' on the event because this seemed to many a universal of communication that held regardless of crosslinguistic differences. The driving question of this research was what exactly 'speakers' viewpoint' could mean. One possible answer was that the speaker's viewpoint is not just 'the speakers'', but is rather a combination of three factors. The first is the part of the event that is relevant for the speaker: its beginning, its duration or its end. The second is how (and for how long) the events unfolds in time, independently of the speaker's standpoint. The third is whether the event occurs simultaneously or in the past or future. Some therefore attempted to define GA by the interaction of three different 'times' in language: (i) the time that is relevant to the speaker's narrative; (ii) the time that is intrinsic to the situation presented (e.g., how the events unfold in the world), and (iii) the time with respect to the moment of utterance. Klein (1994) (following Reichenbach, 1947) called time (i) 'Topic Time' (TT). This is the interval of time from which the event is focalized, or "the time span to which the speaker's claim is confined" (Klein, 1994, p. 6). All that the speaker is assuming about the event – its beginning, its duration and its conclusion – concerns the TT. In contrast, time (ii) is called Situation Time (ST), which represents the interval of time in which the event can occur according to the laws of nature and/or to our knowledge of how the events unfold in the real world. Finally, the Time of the Utterance (TU) places the events in the present, in the past or in the future with respect to the act of speaking/writing (Section 1.3). Klein (1994) defines GA in reference to the special relationship between TT and ST. Let us repeat here the example of sentence (1):

(1) *When Marco looked through the window, he saw Elena watching TV*

In this sentence, the TT is the time from the narrator's perspective. It is the portion of 'look through the window', 'see Elena' and 'watch TV' that is highlighted in order for the story to move on. The ST is the time seen from the standpoint of all the temporal phases that make up the event. These phases can be represented by the reader/hearer independently of the speaker's viewpoint. Likely, 'look through a window' is made of a short preparatory phase and of a longer duration phase, while 'see Elena' is made of two very short phases of directing the gaze and receiving the image on the retina.

The perfective Aspect is used when TT and ST coincide – in our case, when both the initial and the final phase of 'look through the window' and 'see Elena' are made visible by the speaker to the reader/hearer of the sentence. On the other hand, the Imperfective Aspect is when TT is included in ST – in our case, when the initial and the final boundaries of 'watch TV' are left out of sight by the speaker and the event is presented from within ("the time for which an assertion is made falls entirely within the time of the situation"; Klein, 1994, p. 108). And what about the Time of Utterance? The TU signals the relationship holding between the event being described and the time when the sentence is uttered/written. Here, the relevant categories are not only 'present', 'past' and 'future', but also 'perfect' vs. 'nonperfect'. The Perfect is not to be confused with the Perfective. The Perfective indicates that the event is seen from the outside. Perfect means that the event is relevant for (i.e., has consequences for) the TU. A good example of the distinction between the Perfective and the Perfect is provided by English:

(8) *Daniela left her luggage unattended at the station* (simple past, perfective but nonperfect)
(9) *Daniela has left her luggage unattended at the station* (present perfect, perfective and perfect)

In both (8) and (9), the event of Daniela leaving her luggage is situated before the Time of Utterance. The aspectual structure for the simple past is such that the TT in (8) coincides with the final point of the ST. Here the speaker's focus is on the final boundary of the past event of Daniela leaving her luggage unattended. The speaker presents the event as past and completed, leaving completely out of sight its virtual relevance for the TU. Instead, the aspectual structure for the present perfect is such that the TT of event (9) is placed just in coincidence with the TU. Here the speaker's viewpoint is no more placed on the final point of Daniela leaving her luggage unattended, but rather on the possible consequences of her action for the TU. In fact, it is often said that the Perfect is 'deictic', meaning that it has a psychological or causal relevance for the moment in which the sentence is uttered (the TU). A reader of (9) might expect as an optimal completion for the sentence something that sounds like ' . . . and now the police are searching for her'. The different mapping of GA categories onto different verb forms means that in some languages (e.g., Italian) the English present perfect must be translated with the present Tense, like in (10) and (11):

(10) *I have known him for three years* (English present perfect)
(11) *Lo conosco da tre anni* (Italian, present)

In Italian the use of the present Tense emphasizes that the fact of 'having known him for three years' is the prelude of something relevant for the TU (e.g., 'and still I cannot remember his birthday'). The English vs. Italian aspectual mismatch often lures into error even the most expert translators. For instance, in *Star Wars Episode IV: A New Hope*, the Jedi master Obi-Wan Kenobi addresses young Luke Skywalker with the sentence reported in (12). The sentence was translated incorrectly with the past perfective in Italian (13) when the movie was first released in Italy:

(12) *I haven't gone by the name Obi-Wan since before you were born* (English, present perfect)
(13) **Non ho usato / Non uso il nome di Obi-Wan da prima che tu nascessi* (Italian *passato prossimo / present)

These and many other crosslinguistic misalignments between expressions of Aspect and expressions of Tense lead some generative linguists to conclude that Aspect (i.e., GA) is built 'on top' of Tense, because the latter would be subordinate to the former in a speaker's mental grammar (Section 2.4). In example (12), Tense (present vs. past opposition) is subordinate to the expression of GA (relevance vs. nonrelevance for the TU).

1.6 A Famous Aspectual Diagnostic (and Its Problems)

In the last 40 years, many authors of L1 and L2 acquisition studies have relied on their own intuitions or used aspectual diagnostics to code the LAsp (especially the telicity) of predicates. In this tradition, the adverbial modification test has always had a central role. Van Hout et al. (2005, p. 6) wrote that "a large part of the past 40 years has been used to sort out how this test works for Germanic and Romance languages, and which complements of the verb participate in the pattern". In this section, we analyze the adverbial test and list a number of problems that emerge from its application. Such problems become central whenever one tries to define both LAsp and GA.

The adverbial diagnostic was inspired especially by Vendler (1967) and Dowty (1979). Although the latter did not adopt the term 'telicity' in his analysis, he wrote that activity (atelic) and accomplishment (telic) predicates are distinguished by restrictions on the form of time adverbials they can take and by entailments they have when various time adverbial phrases are present. Dowty (1979, p. 56) wrote that "whereas accomplishment verbs [telic] take adverbial prepositional phrases with *in* but only very marginally take adverbial with *for*, activity verbs [atelic] allow only the for-phrases". Sentences 14 a–b and 15 a–b show this contrast:

(14a) ?*John painted a picture for one hour*
(14b) *John painted a picture in one hour*
(15a) *John walked for one hour*
(15b) *John walked in one hour*

An *in* adverbial measures the time span within which eventualities expressed by telic predicates culminate, while a *for* adverbial measures the temporal duration of eventualities denoted by atelic predicates (Filip, 2012, p. 722). Not all authors have deemed adverbial modification a reliable test. Some included it in their collection of diagnostics (e.g., Borer, 2004, p. 294), while others did not (e.g., Andersen & Shirai, 1994). Shirai (2013, p. 288) claimed that time adverbials would often function as a perspective-taker and would obscure the distinction between LAsp and GA. Actually, many L2 studies on Aspect do not use aspectual diagnostics at all. For example, I surveyed a sample of 45 SLA studies published from 1998 to 2018 in peer-reviewed, international journals, conference proceedings and edited volumes. In 24 of those studies (about 53 percent), the authors did not use any diagnostics. Most often, the predicates L2 learners produced/comprehended were simply coded as telic or atelic without further discussion (e.g., Montrul & Slabakova, 2003). Among the 21 SLA studies that utilized aspectual diagnostics, 10 included the adverbial modification test while 11 did not.

The adverbial modification test has a long history, is easy to administer and is probably the most popular aspectual diagnostic. However, it is also problematic. The first challenge when using an adverbial modification test is that it systematically conveys two 'aspectual leaks'. A directional PP (e.g., 'to school') or a bare plural (e.g., 'pictures') suffice to shift the LAsp from atelic to telic and vice versa, respectively, thus rendering English sentences like (16) and (17) acceptable:

(16) *John walked to school in one hour* (TELIC)
(17) *John painted pictures for one hour* (ATELIC)

The second challenge is that telicity has a special relationship with transitive predicates. In accomplishments such as 'build the house', telicity stems from the interaction between the incremental properties of the verb 'build' and the delimitedness in the object NP 'the house'. As we have seen, the eventuality structures of numerous atelic predicates regularly interact with the definiteness of the article and the cardinality-quantifiability (the degree of incrementality) of the direct object. Such interaction determines telicity compositionally (Section 1.4.2). Many languages – English and Italian included – have a large class of transitive verbs that can show both telic and atelic behavior according to the adverbial modification test (e.g., 'the scientist examined the virus in/for an hour'; 'Mum cooked the egg in/for five minutes').

The third challenge – pointed out by Smollet (2005), among others – is that in many cases, semantics, contextual factors and speakers' knowledge of the world codetermine telicity and cause the (in)compatibility of predicates with either time adverbial. For example, in many languages (e.g., Korean, Italian, English) 'inchoative state' or 'degree achievement' predicates corresponding to the English 'cool', 'dry', 'sprout', 'rise' are compatible with either 'in x-time' or 'for x-time' adverbials depending on the trait [±human] of the grammatical subject or on adverbial modification. One can say both 'Mario has aged rapidly in one year' and 'the wine has aged for ten years'. Moreover, depending on whether the agent is human or not (e.g., an ant), the atelic reading of the event 'eat the apple' is more or less acceptable ('the ant/Steve ate the apple for hours'; Smollet, 2005). Some atelic predicates are compatible with in-adverbials when particular NPs suggest the existence of a 'minimal amount' of the event. For example, in the sentence 'Mary is an incredibly fast eater. Yesterday she ate peanuts in 0.43 seconds!' there is an atomic subevent, roughly corresponding to 'eat a handful of peanuts'. This minimal amount of the broader event of 'eating peanuts' creates a culmination point that makes this atelic verb compatible with terminative adverbials (Krifka, 1998, p. 218). Finally, one can always think of a proper context where the object NP – although quantified – did not undergo consumption, like in Smollett's (2005, p. 50) example: 'Becky ate an apple for a couple of minutes while talking on the phone'.

The fourth challenge is related to the way the predicates should be presented in the adverbial test. Some maintain that past morphology – in languages that display the perfective vs. imperfective distinction in the past, such as Italian – should be avoided and that verbs should be presented at the present Tense or at root infinitive. This is because, when reading the predicates at the perfective, speakers may be driven to confound boundedness (pertaining to GA) and telicity/terminativeness (pertaining to LAsp). This issue refers back to a long-standing theoretical stance concerning whether GA and LAsp should (Depraetere, 1995; Bertinetto & Delfitto, 2000) or should not be kept apart, either because perfective morphology inherently instantiates telic events (e.g., Vikner & Vikner, 1997) or because imperfective morphology inherently instantiates atelic events (e.g., Parsons, 1989).

The final challenge is that the adverbial test is perhaps more language-specific than other diagnostics because of the presence of the prepositions *in* and *for*. For example, with negated atelic predicates, even varieties of a single language may behave differently: British English prefers for while American English prefers in (e.g., "I haven't seen you for/in two days"). Other languages may line up in either way: in Swedish a negative atelic predicate gets the same preposition as an affirmative telic one ('på' rather than 'i'), whereas in Russian, negative and affirmative atelics align (null rather than 'za') (Östen Dahl, personal correspondence). Cover & Tonhauser (2015, p. 334) argued that the adverbial test would fail in many non-European languages that lack prepositions (such as Badiaranke, an Atlantic, Niger–Congo language spoken in Senegal, Guinea and Guinea-Bissau). Shirai (2013, p. 276) reported that activity and achievement verbs are easy to distinguish in English but hard to distinguish in Japanese. In Russian and other Slavic languages, delimitative verbs with prefix *po-* are incompatible with both adverbials, so one cannot test these verbs using the adverbial modification diagnostic (Nossalik, 2007). Van Hout et al. (2005, p. 6) stated that for English and other Germanic languages, the test targets LAsp, whereas in Slavic languages it just targets imperfectivity.

1.7 How Children Learn GA

Studies on L1 acquisition have investigated whether and at what age children can map the perfective and imperfective forms onto different perspectives (boundedness vs. unboundedness) on events. Wagner's (2002) study of 59 children (ages 2, 4 and 5) showed that children may not be sensitive to the ±boundedness (event completion) feature of verb morphology until as late as age 5. Wagner (2002) suggested that the degree of intentionality of the agent – and not only the relative completion of the object – may count for children's decisions as to whether imperfective sentences can or cannot refer to bounded events. Kazanina and Phillips (2003, 2007) investigated how Russian children (aged 3–6 years) addressed the issue of event completion in their L1. In one experiment, the authors found that Russian-speaking children incorrectly ascribed completion entailments and boundedness to imperfectives. These children failed to consistently associate the imperfective with incomplete events. In successive experiments, however, the same children recognized that imperfectives could describe incomplete events. Children were facilitated in this task when the imperfective (underlined below) described only a part of the past event that was preceded and delimited by an adverbial sentence (e.g., 'while the boy was watering the flowers the girl was cleaning the table'). Kazanina and Phillips (2007) argued that very young children need a suitable temporal interval against which to evaluate imperfective statements. Since children might find it difficult to associate telic events with the imperfective perspective, the temporal interval provided children with an "explicit insider perspective" (Kazanina & Phillips, 2007, p. 91).

In a broad international project focused on the L1 acquisition of the perfective entailment (meant as the degree of completeness of events), researchers compared the interpretation and production of perfective and imperfective forms in 33 languages in a sample of 266 5-year-old children (Van Hout, 2008a; 2008b). Researchers presented children with a video of a clown performing some actions (e.g., 'build a bridge') while music played. When the music stopped, the clown had to freeze. At this point the children had to tell if a sentence (perfective or imperfective) matched the situation (e.g., 'While the music was playing the clown built / was building a bridge') or complete the sentence with the correct past form, as in the example above. The results showed that the semantic markedness of the [±perfective] forms helped acquisition. In languages in which the [±perfective] shift is overtly marked (e.g., Slavic languages, Italian, Spanish and Basque), children were more likely to recognize perfective entailments. However, children whose L1s assigned telicity through sentence-level computation (e.g., English) were more likely to accept sentences at the perfective describing incomplete situations.

1.8 The Interaction Between LAsp and GA

Much current discussion about Aspect concerns whether or not LAsp and GA are separate (albeit interacting) concepts – and, more specifically, whether event culmination (pertaining to LAsp) and event boundedness (pertaining to GA) should be kept apart. According to the position presented in Section 1.4.2, while culmination is inherent to the predicate's meaning, boundedness is imposed by the speaker's perspective. As we have seen, these two can converge or diverge because TT and ST may or may not coincide. Separateness between these dimensions means that, for example, having stopped drawing a circle (because there has been 'enough of drawing' from the speaker's viewpoint) does not necessarily imply that drawing is completed (that the circle has been drawn). In fact, progressive sentences can present telic events as incomplete, provided that speakers can represent their prolongation and completion in a virtual world which is not focused upon in the sentence. Dowty (1979, p. 148) calls this "inertia world," while Landman (1992, p. 27) uses the expression "continuation branch." Separateness between GA and LAsp is the position held by Smith (1991,

p. 5): "sentences present aspectual information about situation type and viewpoint. Although they co-occur, the two types of information are independent."

At least two positions participate in this debate. One radical claim is that LAsp is totally insensitive to the [±perfective] shift (De Swart, 1998, p. 369). A different position holds that the two levels of aspectual representations are highly interdependent (e.g., Salaberry, 2008; see Sections 1.10 and 2.7) and that the dimensions of boundedness and completeness cannot be kept apart because (a) perfective morphology inherently instantiates telic events (Vikner & Vikner, 1997), (b) imperfective morphology inherently instantiates atelic events (Parsons, 1989), and (c) the perfective past always advances the story in narrative speech, regardless of a predicate's telicity (Kamp & Rohrer, 1983). For the purposes of this section, point (a) is particularly relevant. It accounts for the fact that a shift in [±perfective] morphology alone can turn some predicates from atelic to telic, as shown by the contrast between (18a) and (18b) in Italian (adapted from Bertinetto, 1986, 2001):

(18a) *Martina indossava un bel vestito*
Martina wear3ps (past-IMPERF) a nice dress
'Martina was wearing a nice dress' → **stative (atelic)**

(18b) *Martina ha indossato un bel vestito*
Martina wear3ps (past-PERF.) a nice dress
'Martina wore a nice dress' → **accomplishment (telic)**

In spite of its diffusion, this phenomenon is not so systematic that one could conclude that in Italian LAsp feeds off GA. Yet the phenomenon characterizes a subset of Italian verbs (including *imbracciare il fucile* 'hold the rifle' and *connettere* 'connect') that are atelic at the imperfective and telic at the perfective. Usually, atelic activity predicates such as *dormire* 'sleep', *camminare* 'walk' or *parlare* 'talk' remain so when LAsp morphology shifts. For example, if *dormire* 'sleep' is presented as bounded by using the perfective past, as in sentence (19a):

(19a) *Ho dormito fino alle 9*
(I) haveAUX slept until to the 9
'I slept until 9'

its inherent atelic-ness cannot be erased. In fact, if punctual adverbials are added, such as *in quattro ore* 'in four hours' in sentence (19b),

(19b) ?*Ho dormito in quattro ore*
?'I slept in four hours'

the lack of an endpoint in the LAsp causes the incompatibility between the predicate and the adverbial to surface and the sentence to become odd.

An interesting proposal about the interaction between GA and LAsp was formulated by Salaberry (2008) and Salaberry and Martins (2014). These authors argued that the more context one adds to a given situation, the more the reader/hearer, in order to interpret the sentence, relies on core aspectual values of perfective and imperfective meanings. These 'core aspectual values' are, for instance, those summed up by Binnick (1991): "[t]he imperfect(ive) has continual, habitual, and generic uses in many languages, while the perfect(ive) has punctual, iterative, and resultative uses" (p. 156). In contrast, the *less* contextualized the situation is, the more likely it is that selections of perfective and imperfective markings will be guided by prototypical selections (Section 2.2) and by frequency. Essentially, the richer the contextual information a reader/hearer must take into account, the more likely GA and LAsp values are to be computed separately and to contribute separately – but distinctly – to the interpretation of the sentence.

1.9 Aspect Crosslinguistically

There exist dozens of papers and books about crosslinguistic variation in the domain of GA. Much less has been written about how LAsp is encoded in different languages. For example, LAsp – unlike GA – is featured neither in the World Atlas of Language (Dryer & Haspelmath, 2013), nor on the list of distinguishing features of SAE languages in the EUROTYP project (Haspelmath, 2001), nor in recent reviews about semantic universals (e.g., Chao & Bach, 2009). For this reason, in this section we focus on analyzing the understudied but extremely revealing crosslinguistic variation in the domain of LAsp.

Let us start from an apparent paradox. Although the event 'die' is presumably the same all over the world (the experience of death is shared among all humans), different languages conceptualize the LAsp of the predicates corresponding to the event 'die' in very different ways. Botne (2003) compared 'die' verbs in 18 languages. He first observed that 'die' is typically classified as an achievement verb in English, along with other verbs such as 'find', 'notice' and 'recognize'. He quoted Binnick (1991, p. 195): "An achievement is all culmination; though the achievement is possibly preceded by some activity . . . the verb refers only to the achievement phase, not to the preceding activity." Achievements like 'die' should therefore have no duration. This is because all achievements such as 'reach (summit)', 'find', 'notice' have a punctual nucleus and cannot co-occur with expressions such as 'in the midst of', which require a durative nucleus (Botne, 2003, p. 80). Instead, the author in his review found that "while the crucial and core aspect of this event is the pivotal transition point demarcating life and death, verbs (or adjectives) refer not to the original fact of life, but to various stages in the process of change leading to death" (p. 81). For example, in this analysis Botne (2003) found that English, Arabic, Hausa and French encode in 'die' a durative onset phase plus a punctual nucleus (like in English 'he was dying' or in Egyptian Arabic *bi-y-muut* 'he's dying'). In contrast, the Japanese verb *sinu* cannot refer to such an onset phase of dying, because it encodes a stative coda phase (the resulting state of being dead). To sum up, Botne (2003) counted up to four types of 'die' verbs in his sample of world languages: acute achievement (focusing on the very crucial instant), inceptive (focusing on the time before dying), resultative (focusing on the interval after dying) and transitional (focusing on the passage from life to death). This is probably not enough to conclude that Vendlerian aspectual classes are not valid crosslinguistically, but it suggests that any aspectual comparisons can be done only if all the elements of the sentence are considered, and not only the verb.

Let us now focus on how Slavic, Romance, Germanic and Sino-Tibetan (Mandarin Chinese) families encode LAsp. This is particularly important from the language acquisition perspective, as we will see in Section 2. Under the 'syntactic approaches' to telicity (Section 2.4), many authors have focused on the structural opposition between Germanic and Slavic languages (see Filip, 2004; Ayoun & Rothman, 2013 for a review). Two different sources of telicity are relevant for comparing those families: a dedicated functional projection above the VP (variously called AspP, ASPquantity, AgrOP; see van Hout, 2004, p. 61; Borer, 2004, p. 294; see also Section 2.4) and the presence of a telicity feature (quantifiers, definite article and accusative case) in the direct object determiner phrase (DO-DP). The difference between Slavic and Germanic languages lies in what triggers the aspectual derivation and determines the specifier–head relationship.

In Germanic languages, the presence of any telicity features in the DO-DP raises it to the specifier position of the functional head AspP. Therefore, the presence of a definite article or the expression of a defined quantity (as opposed to bare plurals) will trigger a telic interpretation. In Slavic languages, as we have seen, verb morphology within the VP triggers its telic interpretation and binds the DO-DP as specifier of its head. Therefore, the presence of the perfective prefix will cause the verb to become telic.

Extensive research on L1 acquisition has shown that telicity is easier to learn when it is overtly marked (as in Slavic languages) rather when it must be computed from the properties of the VP and its object together (as in Germanic languages) (van Hout, 2008a). To our knowledge, there are no similar studies concerning L2 acquisition by adult learners. In theory, at least, if speakers of Slavic languages can more easily recognize telic verbs in their first language, they could face problems making such distinctions in languages where telicity is covert (e.g., Italian or Spanish). As noted in Section 1.2, Slavic languages use preverbal morphemes to indicate perfective Aspect; null suffixes indicate that an event is ongoing (Slabakova, 2001, p. 5). Many authors maintain that these morphemes conflate [+telic] and [+perfective] values, which therefore cannot be easily disentangled. In Italian, there is no systematic conflation between LAsp and GA (for a very similar situation in Spanish, see Montrul, 2002, p. 42).

In Mandarin Chinese, Aspect is coded by four free morphemes, which do not express tenses but, rather, different perspectives on the situation. Particles *zhe* and *zai* characterize the situation as imperfective, progressive or durative, whereas *le* and *guo* express a perfective Aspect (Li & Thompson, 1981). Since it is not entirely clear whether aspectual markers in Chinese encode just GA or also its interaction with LAsp (Klein et al. 2000), learning that such dimensions in Italian, Spanish or French are separate could take time and additional effort for L1 Chinese learners.

Of course, typological families are not monolithic. For example, within the Slavic family, Bulgarian has articles while Russian and Czech do not. This may affect learners' sensitivity to the existence of a delimiting feature in the DO-DP (Di Sciullo & Slabakova, 2005). As another example, L1 Cantonese speakers are used to a richer and phonologically more salient aspectual system than Mandarin speakers (Matthews & Yip, 2013, chapter 11).

1.10 The Pragmatic Correlate of Aspect: Aspectual Coercion

A sentence like (20) looks odd or even unacceptable:

(20) ?*Ho dormito in cinque minuti*
I sleptPERF in five minutes

because *dormire* 'sleep' is lacking an endpoint and is therefore incompatible with punctual adverbials such as in x-time. The sentence shows a conflict between LAsp and GA. In some cases, this conflict is remediable through a mechanism called 'aspectual coercion' (or 'type shift'), which is available in a native speaker's competence. Aspectual coercion is governed by implicit, contextual reinterpretation mechanisms (of pragmatic, syntactic and semantic nature) which are triggered by the need to resolve aspectual conflicts (De Swart, 1998). For instance, in Spanish the verb *saber* ('know') is stative, but it can be shifted to the meaning of acquiring knowledge, which is telic (*supe* 'I found out'; see Salaberry, 2008). Also, sentence (16) would become at least slightly more acceptable if the predicate 'sleep' could be reinterpreted as 'fall asleep', like in (21):

(21) *I fell asleep in five minutes*

As another example, when reading a sentence like (22),

(22) *Bruce Springsteen played his last album for one year*

an English native speakers (NS) automatically reinterprets the event of 'play an album' as an iterated activity (e.g. playing in concerts) even though the predicate 'plays his last album' is an accomplishment and as such includes a result phase in its event structure. NSs know that most predicates may have multiple actional interpretations depending on the context. Another famous example of aspectual coercion is reported by Gvozdanović (2012, p. 2):

(23) *He wrote a letter for two hours, then he decided not to finish it*

This sentence is acceptable provided that the focus of the interpretation is not on the resulting phase (the letter being written) but on the process.

A speaker's knowledge of the world and of the laws of nature may also conspire with all the linguistic elements of the VP to coerce the features of GA toward an acceptable interpretation. Let us consider the conditions of compatibility between the Italian gerundive periphrasis – an imperfective-progressive form – and two punctual, achievement verbs: *starnutire* 'sneeze' and *esplodere* 'explode'. In Section 1.4, we said that the progressive-imperfective presents the event from within. One is justified in doubting that *starnutire* 'sneeze' and *esplodere* 'explode' last long enough to be represented in their duration phase. Yet sentences (24) and (25) are perfectly acceptable in Italian:

(24) *Daniela sta starnutendo* [IMPERFECTIVE] *molto*
Daniela is sneezing a lot

(25) *La bomba sta esplodendo* [IMPERFECTIVE]
The bomb is exploding

In order for sentence (24) to become meaningful, an Italian native speaker will likely represent multiple sneezes in a sequence, so that 'Daniela is sneezing' refers to an iterative rather than to a punctual event ('Daniele keeps on sneezing'). In order for sentence (25) to become meaningful, a native Italian speaker will likely focus on the impending phase of the event, so that 'the bomb is exploding' becomes inchoative ('the bomb is about to explode'). More technically, it is said that coercion indicates "a modular grammatical architecture, in which the process of semantic composition may add meanings absent from the syntax in order to ensure that certain operators, e.g., the progressive, receive suitable arguments" (Michaelis, 2004, p. 1). Aspectual coercion requires not only compositionality (codetermination of Aspect at VP level; Section 1.4.5), but also an interpolation of extra meaning – a totally invisible operation on the part of the speaker/hearer – that Jackendoff (1997) calls "enriched composition".

1.11 To Sum Up

In this section, we discussed the reasons why Aspect can be considered a 'multifaceted property of predicates', with syntactic, semantic and pragmatic correlates. On the one hand, we have seen that all elements of the verb surrounding – the subject, the object and the adjuncts – interact in complex ways in order to define its aspectual category. On the other hand, we insisted on the need to disentangle verb semantics (which pertains to language) and ontology (which pertains to how the mind conceives how events unfold in the world). Finally, we recognized that aspectual categories are not rigid and that speakers have the pragmatic competence and means to overcome the boundaries among such categories during language comprehension. In Section 2 we move to the domain of second language acquisition (SLA). When interpreting L2 data, SLA researchers are generally aware that L2 Aspect is even more difficult to pin down because the syntactic, semantic and pragmatic constraints that make up the meaning of the predicate operate on features that are still in reconstruction in a learner's competence.

2 What Are the Implications for SLA?

The acquisition of L2 Aspect is without a doubt one the most investigated issues in the history of SLA research (for a recent meta-analysis of studies, see Bardovi-Harlig & Comajoan-Colomé, 2020). One famous hypothesis proposed to explain the acquisition of L2 Aspect is known as the 'Lexical Aspect Hypothesis' (LAH). This section describes its fundamental tenets, compares its various versions, examines the methodology and the data supporting it and finally considers the criticism that this hypothesis has provoked.

When introducing the nonspecialist reader to the LAH, one piece of information is necessary. Over the last three decades, at least the basic tenets of the LAH have reached a cross-theoretical consensus which has perhaps no equal in any other SLA theory. In spite of their differences, many scholars – even those from opposite orientations – came to agree with the principle that LAsp (namely, the telic vs. atelic opposition) is what ultimately determines how and at what rate L2 learners acquire the opposition between perfective and imperfective Aspect.

Such agreement is so widespread that nowadays the basic tenets of the LAH are considered mainstream and, some would say, 'textbook wisdom' in many conferences, journal papers and monographies.

2.1 The Lexical Aspect Hypothesis

2.1.1 Background: L1 Acquisition

The LAH was preceded and prepared by the observation that children learning their first language can represent aspectual categories (especially boundedness and telicity) before they can represent temporal relations (present, past and future) between the events and the TU. Antinucci and Miller (1976) examined longitudinal conversational data from seven Italian-speaking children and one English-speaking child (ages 1;6 to 2;5). They noticed that these children used the Italian bare past participle (without the auxiliary) only with telic verbs (e.g., *venire* 'come', *arrivare* 'arrive') but not with stative verbs (e.g., *volere* 'want', *sapere* 'know') or activity verbs (e.g., *volare* 'fly', *camminare* 'walk'). Antinucci and Miller concluded that children mark events with past verbal morphology only if such events have a resulting state – that is, only if the event described by the verb led to a change that affected the subject or the object (p. 182). For example, children will use past perfective verbal morphology (the *passato prossimo*) with the verbs *venire* 'come' and *arrivare* 'arrive' not because they want to express the idea that the event is in the past but because those verbs express a directed motion event and they can visualize the end of that motion in their event structure (Pusteiovski, 1991).

Another famous example is the Italian short sentence *rotto giocattolo* (lit. 'broken-toy') uttered by an Italian child of the corpus CHILDES. This sentence should not be interpreted as referring to an event situated in the past (e.g., 'the toy broke') but rather as indicating the end-state of *rompere* 'break' which is relevant for the present (something like 'the toy is broken'). In sum, children would not use early past morphology to encode temporal relations they cannot master yet, but the outcome state of a process (e.g., being here, turning yellow, becoming old, arriving home, hammer the copper flat, etc.).

Similar results were described by Brockert and Sinclair (1973), who analyzed the sentences produced by 74 French-speaking children (ages 2;11 to 8;7). These authors found that before the age of 6 children mostly used perfective past forms (the French *passé composé*) for telic events and present forms (the French *présent*) for durative, atelic events. When children begin to extend the use of *passé composé* to all events, usually around the age of six, then they probably can also use verbal morphology to express Tense.

In the 1980s and 1990s, other hypotheses that highlighted the developmental priority of Aspect over Tense emerged in L1 acquisition studies: the 'Aspect before Tense hypothesis' (Bloom et al., 1980), the 'defective Tense hypothesis' (Weist et al., 1984) and the 'Aspect first hypothesis' (Wagner, 2001).

2.1.2 The LAH

The LAH was proposed by Roger Andersen and Yasuhiro Shirai in the early 1990s, but it is mainly based on data collected in the 1980s concerning Spanish acquired naturally as a second language by English-speaking children living in Puerto Rico (especially by Anthony, a twelve-year-old native speaker of English). Andersen observed that the Spanish *pretérito simple* (perfective) inflection (such as *–ó* in *cayó* 'fell') appeared initially only on achievement verbs, then later also on accomplishments, then spread to activities and finally to states (e.g., *estuvo* 'was'). Andersen also noticed that learners of L2 Spanish did not use the *imperfecto* at all for a long time. First uses of the *imperfecto* were on states (e.g., *sabía* 'knew', *estaba* 'was') and then with activity verbs (e.g., *jugaba* 'played', *pintaba* 'painted'), spreading later to accomplishments and to achievements.

The LAH, which derived from these and other observations and has become canonical over the years, comprises three separate but interconnected claims (Andersen & Shirai, 1996, p. 533):

A. Learners first use past marking (e.g., English) or perfective marking (e.g., Chinese, Spanish, etc.) on achievements and accomplishment verbs, eventually extending its use to activities and then to stative verbs;
B. In languages that encode the perfective/imperfective distinction, a morphologically encoded imperfective past (as in Romance languages) appears later than perfective past, and imperfective past marking begins with stative and activity verbs, then extends to accomplishment or achievement verbs;
C. In languages that have progressive Aspect, progressive marking begins with activity verbs, then extends to accomplishment and achievement verbs.

According to the LAH, LAsp affects the acquisition of Tense-Aspect morphology because L2 learners acquire temporal-aspectual morphemes selectively. The emergence of the past (in English) and of perfective marking (e.g., French, Italian, Spanish, Chinese) in adult L2 learners would be initially limited to telic (achievement and accomplishment) verbs such as 'went to school', 'fell down', 'brought', 'broke' (Shirai & Andersen, 1995, table 7). If L2 learners' knowledge of LAsp truly modulates the pace of L2 acquisition of aspectual morphemes, then in L2 Italian, for example, the perfective *passato prossimo* morphemes would be first associated with telic and later with atelic verbs, while the opposite would hold for the *imperfetto*. It is important to remember that the LAH states that only the early emergence of perfective and imperfective morphology would be constrained by LAsp. At subsequent stages of L2 acquisition, verb morphology spreads to all LAsp categories (even if the spread of imperfective morphology from atelic to telic predicates seems not to be equally well attested; see Bardovi-Harlig, 2000).

It is important to stress what the LAH does and does *not* predict. First, the LAH poses a developmental priority of Aspect over Tense. As Salaberry (2011, p. 184) puts it: "the use of past tense inflectional markers reaffirms primarily the lexical aspectual value of the verb phrase, and secondarily conveys information about tense or grammatical aspect." Second, as Andersen (2002, p. 82) puts it: "the Aspect Hypothesis does not predict that just any token of an achievement verb .... will automatically attract a perfective marker, but rather that when the marker is used, it will be used more often with achievements (or perhaps with telic events in general) than with verbs of other semantic properties (activities and states)." The LAH is in fact made of two quite different components. The one quoted by Andersen is the *descriptive (probabilistic) component*: the data from different languages seems to converge, showing that LAsp influences the acquisition of the L2 Tense-Aspect system in predictable ways. The other component of the LAH is the *explanatory component*. This component searches for the principles that drive L2 learners to rely on LAsp when making their way through L2 Tense-Aspect morphology. Most scholars agree on the former component (the description) but disagree on the latter (the explanations). Shirai (2016) sums up that there has been general agreement on the predicted association patterns as a universal tendency, whereas explanations for these tendencies are still controversial (Section 3.5). Shirai identifies two competing explanations: the input-based explanation (the 'Distributional Bias Hypothesis') and the nativist explanation proposed by generative scholars. Actually, in Sections 2.2–2.7 we count up to five different accounts of the data that have been proposed to support the LAH over the last 30 years.

2.1.3 Where Did the LAH Come From?

Like many other SLA hypotheses, the LAH was the result of combined insights from psychological theories that were very popular in the 1970s and '80s, especially among nongenerative linguists. Roger Andersen was particularly inspired by the early work of Dan Slobin. According to Slobin, the ways in which the human mind perceives, organizes and puts into hierarchies the information received from the input determines the pace and rate at which languages are learned by both children and adults. The basic claim is that certain linguistic forms are *naturally* more accessible and more salient than others because the ways in which they appear and are organized conform better to some universal cognitive principles, which make learning easier. Slobin listed a number of such 'operating principles' that explain why some forms are processed and learned first and more efficiently (Slobin, 1979). For example, one principle states that underlying semantic relations that are marked overtly and clearly are learned first. The corresponding language acquisition universal is that the closer a grammatical system adheres to one-to-one mapping between semantic elements (e.g., verb meaning) and surface elements (e.g., past morphemes) the earlier it will be acquired. This principle predicts, for example, that initial learners will tend to avoid polysemy and multifunctionality and will always prefer mapping one meaning onto just one form (and the other way round). Andersen (1984) adapted this and other operating principles to SLA. Andersen's one-to-one principles states that, in a learner's interlanguage, one will likely find that a given meaning will be expressed by just one clear invariant surface form or construction rather than by an array of different forms. It is easy to see the connection between this idea and the general idea that, in order to express the meaning of the past, initial learners will overextend just one form (the perfective) to contexts where the imperfective would be expected.

Another principle is the 'principle of distributional bias'. This states that initial learners will restrict the meaning of a given form to the contexts in which this form appears more frequently. Again, the link between this idea and the LAH is evident. If an L2 learner encounters the perfective morpheme almost exclusively with a limited set of telic verb lexemes, she will tend to interpret the perfective as an exclusive and inherent marker of those lexemes. L2 learners would therefore be reluctant to detach the morpheme from prototypical verbs and to extend it to all the available verbal lexicon. This principle in particular obeys a more general cognitive learning principle called 'contingency learning'. Contingency learning is a probability-based mechanism for learning whether relations between events are causal or noncausal (Beckers et al., 2007). Speakers and learners tend to label co-occurring events as noncausal when the probability P of getting an outcome O (e.g., thunder) given a cue C (e.g., lightning) ($P(O|C)$) is very high. Noncausal cue–outcome relationships, once identified, trigger category formation. Categories are formed when learners first group co-occurring events (e.g., words) based on adjacency and then assign these events category membership based on noncausal relationships (Reeder et al., 2010). In first and second language acquisition, contingency learning exploits the frequent co-occurrence between a lexeme and a grammatical construction (Goldberg, 2006). The LAH predicts that contingency learning occurs because L2 learners realize that telicity – a semantic feature of the verb lexeme – and the perfective construction are a close match. This is the topic of the next section.

2.2 The Prototype Account

According to the prototype account, there exist clusters of semantically congruent Tense-Aspect and LAsp features that at first are more likely to be associated with each other in L1 and L2 learners' early predicates, then gradually disentangle and finally operate separately as learners progress in their competence of the target language. Shirai and Andersen (1995) claim that the distribution of aspectual morphemes across LAsp categories is biased by an inner predisposition that leads learners to first acquire and use traits that are semantically close or 'congruent'. These congruent traits are pastness, perfectivity and telicity on the one side, and nonpastness, imperfectivity and atelicity on the other.

The idea of congruency stems from L1 studies and reflects the intuition that some associations may be more 'prototypical' than others and that prototypical associations have primacy in both L1 and L2 acquisition: "Children acquire a linguistic category starting with the prototype of the category, and later expand its application to less prototypical cases" (Shirai & Andersen, 1995, p. 758). 'Prototype' is a model of human categorization which was proposed by psychologists independently of second language acquisition (Taylor, 1989) and is widely accepted in functional typology (Dahl, 1985). Prototype theory (Rosch, 1975) was originally put forth to explain how certain members (e.g., oranges) of a category (e.g., fruit) are regarded as more central than other members (e.g., olives). Additionally, some associations between Tense-Aspect morphology and some LAsp categories may be more or less prototypical: in language acquisition, telic predicates would associate prototypically with the past Tense and the perfective morpheme because their most relevant phase is the final one. Since inherent endpoint, boundedness and past align, telic verbs will tend to be presented in the perfective past (e.g., in the Italian *passato prossimo* or the Spanish *pretérito simple*) more easily than atelic verbs. Telic predicates are also more congruent with the perfective Aspect than with the imperfective because in the former, the 'result phase' (Section 1.4.2) – the most relevant phase in telic predicates' event structure – is actualized and augmented just by the presence of the perfective morpheme. For instance, the result phase in the meaning of a telic predicate such as the Italian *cadere* and the Spanish *caer* 'fall' is actualized and put in the proper perspective especially when the event is bounded in the perfective past (*è caduto* '(it) fell') rather than when it is ongoing and incomplete in the imperfective (*sta cadendo* '(it) is falling') or in the present (*cade*'(it) falls'). Prototypical form-meaning associations would be acquired first because learners perceive them as more natural and congruent. As we will see in the next section, prototypical associations are claimed to be simpler to learn than nonprototypical associations (Shirai & Andersen, 1995, p. 758) also because they are reinforced by the distribution of form–function mappings in the input.

Prototypicality is a broad concept that also concerns the acquisition of languages that do not display the perfective vs. imperfective opposition in the past. Let us take English, for example. According to Giorgi and Pianesi (1997), many English verbs are 'naked' forms that can express several values. Moreover, some verbal forms cannot be distinguished from nouns. The authors propose that what distinguishes verbs from nouns is just the feature [+perfective]. A native speaker of English would always represent a verb by default as perfective (completed), whereas the progressive would be the marked, nondefault option. Let us now hypothesize how an L2 learner of English would associate a cluster of prototypical semantic properties (LAsp categories) with past vs. progressive/present when learning L2 English verb morphology. English past forms will be likely automatically assigned the features [+telic] [–durative] [+result], while the English present and progressives will likely be automatically assigned the features [–telic] [+durative] [–result]. Bertinetto and Noccetti (2006) maintain that this would be the result of a probabilistic tendency and that both the child and the older L2 learner may find this correlation in the input and may be naturally inclined to assume that this belongs to the very nature of language. As a consequence, the learner/child would use the different Tense and Aspect morphemes only with verbs exhibiting the prototypical LAsp features. Only later on, and gradually, would s/he learn how to generalize the given morphemes to other verbs, which appear to be peripheral with respect to the semantic prototype. Of course, one may wonder where prototypes come from and how they are formed in the child's mind or in the L2 learner's mind. Andersen (2002, p. 81) suggests that there exists a "natural predisposition" to access the prototypical meaning of a verb. This predisposition would enhance a learner's tendency to initially restrict the early use of Tense-morphology only to a subset of the predicates in a learner's lexicon.

The prototype account has evident shortcomings. First, it cannot account for important exceptions and unexpected, nonprototypical matching between stative and activity verbs with perfective markings that are frequently found in both L1 and L2 corpora. Bertinetto and Noccetti (2006) observed that the activity verb *vedere* 'see' and *disegnare* 'draw' are among the first verbs to be marked with the past participle suffix by Italian children. Analysis of Italian learner languages (Giacalone Ramat, 1995) also confirms that activity predicates often emerged with perfective marking, contrary to the predictions of the LAH. The second shortcoming is that, in general, the emergence of the perfective prototype in learner languages is often delayed because early verbs, regardless of telicity, appear in a present-like form also when a clear past meaning would be expected. Therefore, one would likely find few instances of perfective and imperfective past in early learners' productions – maybe too few instances to conclude anything about an initial learner's competence. The third and most important shortcoming is that the prototype account is at risk of confounding the cause for its consequences. In fact, L2 learners could associate early perfective marking first with telic verbs just because this form-meaning association is the most frequent in the target language input. If this is the case, we expect the distribution of morpheme–lexeme association in L2 data and in L1 data to be the same.

2.3 The Distributional Account

The observation concerning the relationship between frequency in the L1 input and early perfective marking in L2 acquisition of Aspect came to be known as 'the input problem'. As an example, the Italian predicate *uscire* 'go out' – although not particularly frequent in absolute in the L1 input – co-occurs with exceptional frequency with Italian perfective constructions, especially with the inflected forms of the compound past perfective (the *passato prossimo* – e.g., *è uscito* '(he) went out'). In fact, perfective forms of *uscire* 'exit' are significantly more frequent in the L1 input than all nonperfective forms (imperfective, present, conditional, infinitive, etc.) combined. Exactly the same distribution can be found in Italian learner corpora, where the perfective form of *uscire* alone is much more frequent than all nonperfective forms altogether. Given this situation, one may wonder whether L2 learners using the telic predicate *uscire* exclusively at the perfective past are driven by a cognitive principle (as stated by the proponents of the prototype account) or are just mimicking the input. If prototypical associations in L2 data are the same as those in the L1 input, then learners could have absorbed the preferred perfective-telic association just from the input. If L2 learners are simply mimicking an input distribution, one cannot say that they are driven by a cognitive principle. What needs to be clarified is the relationship between distributional properties of the input and universals of cognition: what comes first?

The proposed solution to this puzzle, especially in usage-based, emergentist and connectionist linguistics, is that the competition between input distribution and cognition does not necessarily imply there is a winner. For example, the 'Distributional Bias Hypothesis' described by Shirai and Andersen (1995) and

Andersen (2002) maintains that the cognitive principle of prototypicality *reinforces* a tendency in the input (and the other way round), both in the L1 and in the L2. Researchers then focused on detecting significant deviations between the learners and the native speakers in order to prove that, although the native speakers' speech shares some features with that of learners, the overlap is incomplete. Shirai (2002, p. 459) argues that the predictions of the LAH are not purely dependent on learners' mimicking the input. Yet, L2 learners would be driven by cognitive principles to create semantic representations that are more selectively restricted than native speakers'. Studies would demonstrate that the omission or overuse of verbal morphology in inappropriate contexts is not generalized to all LAsp categories, but rather is limited to prototypical pairings. For example, uninflected forms (where past morphology would be expected) are used more frequently with atelic predicates, while overextension of past forms (where nonpast forms would be expected) is more frequent with telic predicates (for a discussion, see Rohde, 2002, pp. 214–216; Housen, 2002, pp. 179–180). Selective overextensions – as a developmental cognitive strategy – would demonstrate that learners' sensitivity to the prototype account conspires with the distributional bias rather than simply originating from it. Moreover, Andersen (1993, p. 320) suggests that "the native and the learner distributions are both due to the same factors." This means that native speakers and L2 learners show the same distributional tendencies because the same principle of congruence operates for both learners and native speakers alike. Bardovi-Harlig (2012, p. 16) observes that "the frequency account leaves open the question of what underlying (linguistic) principles frequency patterns are based on. The distribution of Tense-Aspect morphology does not come from frequency itself but rather from form-meaning associations that are available from the input, and also from the temporal semantics that underpin them." We agree with this important observation: frequency in the input could well be the consequence, but not the only explanation of prototypical associations. The fact that both factors – frequency and prototype – are often invoked in the literature as explanations for the LAH raises an important theoretical problem of circularity (Section 3.5). This problem has been neither resolved, nor acknowledged and debated as it deserves.

In the emergentist approach to the LAH (Li & Bowermann, 1998; Li & Shirai, 2000; Li, 2002), it is stressed that the early associations between aspectual morphemes and LAsp categories are above all a consequence of learners' implicit capacity to analyze and record the probability of co-occurrence of forms and meanings in the input they are exposed to. As noted, perfective morphemes are most often associated with telic verbs in the input. The frequency of these co-occurrences activates a number of dynamic, adaptive-associative patterns (gradually more and more generalizable), which in turn provide the ground for shaping the semantic categories underlying the four Vendlerian classes (Li, 2000, p. 309). The semantic categories of LAsp would emerge as a result of a bottom-up, non–rule-driven process of acquisition (Li, 2002, p. 84). L2 learners would acquire the telic/atelic distinction because frequent associations reinforce a critical number of neural networks. These neural networks instantiate the LAsp categories in a speaker's and a learner's mental grammar. The prototypical associations are therefore both determined top-down and reinforced bottom-up – that is, statistically (Sections 3.3; 4.2).

2.4 The Syntactic Account

Scholars adopting a syntactic approach to the acquisition of L2 Aspect are less interested in cognitive, general-domain principles such as congruence or prototypicality. To them, such principles are at most secondary and derivative. Moreover, generative scholars often demote the importance of and/or do not adequately operationalize the frequency factor in their studies. On the contrary, traditionally two things really count for syntacticians when explaining how L1 and L2 learners acquire the Tense-Aspect morphology. One is the number and kind of syntactic configurations a verb may enter (if the verb can be transitive or intransitive, unaccusative or unergative, pronominal, reflexive, etc.). The other is the 'verb constellation' – that is, the number and nature of its direct or indirect arguments and also adjuncts, both at VP and (more rarely) sentence level. In spite of these and other differences, most generative scholars agree with cognitive linguists that the fundamental tenet of the LAH –, that is, that LAsp (the telic vs. atelic contrast) – selectively affects the acquisition of Tense-Aspect morphology. However, the explanations proposed are of a different kind. In the generative framework, learners' knowledge of LAsp is derived neither from cognitive, general-domain principles (such as congruence and prototypicality) nor from frequency of lexeme–morpheme associations in the input. Rather, for many generative scholars, telicity is a formal (nonlexical) and interpretable (having semantic content) feature ('φ-feature') hosted and construed in a dedicated functional head called AspP (Aspect Phrase). According to this view, the distinction between telic and atelic predicates is innate rather than learned or derived bottom-up from the input. When exposed to the target-language input, L2 learners – who have innate knowledge of Aspect – are left with the task of finding out how the target language encodes aspectual categories in its predicates. This amounts to discovering which elements (specifiers and complements) fill the various levels of the AspP head in the target language. More recent generative approaches also stress that acquisition of the Tense-Aspect system is dependent on factors that lie at the interface between syntax, morphology, semantics and discourse/pragmatics. Under this latter perspective, aspectual features are represented and processed at the interface between these domains, and their properties are 'interface-conditioned properties' at all effects (Ayoun & Rothman, 2013, p. 120).

Let us first start with a brief historical recap and then focus on the syntactic device – the AspP functional head – whose functioning justifies and explains the acquisition of L2 Aspect. In the early 1990s, Aspect – both GA and LAsp – started to play a major role in generative syntactic theories. At that time the main issue was determining the extent to which the aspectual properties (mainly telicity) of the verb affected (or were affected by) its argument structure. There are two opposing positions: (a) Aspect (essentially, LAsp) determines the syntactic configuration of a verb; (b) the syntactic configuration of a verb (its argument structure) determines Aspect. Among the syntactically relevant aspectual properties were 'affectedness' (the property of an argument undergoing a change of state), 'delimitedness' (the fact that an event is bounded over time) and 'definiteness' (the fact that the direct object NP can be measured, e.g., 'eat sandwiches' vs. 'eat a sandwich'). The view that predicates' LAsp determines syntax was prevalent in the study of resultative constructions, verb-particle constructions and the so-called 'middle' constructions in English. Also, the aspectual properties of the external and internal arguments (in particular, the presence of volitional activity or of a change of state affecting the grammatical subject) were used to account for the unaccusative/unergative behavior of verbs (e.g., Levin & Rappaport, 1995; McClure, 2003; Sorace, 2004). The opposite view was that syntax determines predicates' aspectual properties (for instance Borer, 2004). In this perspective, the structural representation of a given verb (e.g., being transitive, intransitive, unaccusative, unergative, etc.), and not its lexical meaning, is responsible for the aspectual classification. Predicates belong to different LAsp categories (e.g., being telic or atelic) not because of their inherent semantics, but because they have different argument structures. Let us consider the English verb 'fly'. Depending on the preposition, the number and the nature of its arguments, the verb 'fly' can be telic or atelic. In fact, one can say 'yesterday she flew to NYC in two hours' (telic) or 'yesterday she flew over NYC for two hours'. Here prepositions 'to' and 'over' change the scene of the verb – that is, its argument structure. A different argument structure results in a different LAsp category.

Slabakova (2001) put forth a strong claim for L2 acquisition of Aspect playing a central role in the generative theoretical framework. According to her view, the Universal Grammar (UG) – the initial state of or biological endowment for language – forms the basis of the functional categories of

LAsp, which in turn shape four surface-templates corresponding to the four Vendlerian classes. Slabakova (2001) in particular states that telicity is a parameter whose value is learned by children in L1 acquisition and must be set again by adult learners in L2 acquisition. As a parameter, telicity represents a universal semantic construct that is expressed in all languages, albeit in different ways. Essentially, L2 learners are predisposed to receive from the input the information about which semantic value, [±telic], should be set for each predicate. Since the LAsp heads would be functional heads, to all intents and purposes, learners would have privileged, direct and 'once and for all' access to the LAsp content of verbs. Every time a learner thinks of a target-language verb, she will also automatically try to discover whether this verb is telic or atelic. This would also mean that once one aspectual parameter is set for a certain L2 predicate, learners would know which structural properties are associated with that predicate – that is, they would know which configurations a verb is or is not allowed to enter and with which temporal frameworks (e.g., in x-time or for x-time; see Section 1.6) it is compatible.

More technically, Slabakova's claim is based on the structural approach to Aspect developed in Travis (1994, 2010). Travis claims that the four Vendlerian templates of LAsp are generated in between the VP shell structure. The 'VP shell' – the internal structure of the VP – is a convention signaling that when a speaker or a learner thinks of a predicate, she not only computes the relationship between the V and the object NP but also other semantic features, like theta-roles or, in this case, LAsp. Between the higher V_1P and the lower V_2P there are two specifier positions of the functional head AspP that are particularly important. The values of features hosted in these positions codetermine the result of the aspectual computation and, ultimately, whether a verb is telic or not. The lowest specifier position ($AspP^i$) is where the speaker/learner computes whether the direct object is ±definite. The higher position (specifier of V^i) is where the speaker/learner computes whether or not the event is also a process. L2 learners, like native speakers, allegedly project all the lexical information (all they represent about a given verb) onto the syntactic tree – that is, they can supposedly compute all elements within this VP shell structure (between VP_1 and VP_2) and check some of them at the specifier position of AspP to express telicity. Since predicates' lexical properties are encoded in the syntax, the main task for L2 learners is to recognize which target language features (e.g., bare plurals DPs, quantified object DPs, PP, AdvP) should be checked in AspP spec position to express telicity.

Finally, let us return to the important point that the main tenets of the LAH are accepted also in generative linguistics, even if the explanation differs from that proposed by nongenerative scholars. In a series of studies, Roumyana Slabakova and Silvina Montrul (e.g., Slabakova & Montrul, 2000, 2002), found that near-native competence is possible in the domain of aspectual interpretations and that the acquisition of semantics precedes the acquisition of verb morphology. Slabakova (2006) concluded that "the formal features associated with the functional category AspP are acquirable and 'unimpaired' in SLA" (p. 141). This means not only that L2 learners can acquire Aspect, but also that LAsp likely paves the way for the acquisition of Tense-Aspect morphology. Importantly, what generative linguists also found in their studies is that prototypical associations have primacy in acquisition because semantics and aspectual distinctions come for free (i.e., they are built into an L2 learner's mental grammar). This conclusion is similar to that formulated by cognitive, nongenerative linguists.

Behavioral studies conducted by generative linguists seem to confirm this hypothesis. For example, Montrul (2009) found that the Spanish *pretérito simple* (the perfective past) "emerges and is controlled first with accomplishments and achievements, both telic predicates, while imperfect appears first with states and activities, the atelic classes. Extension of *pretérito* to atelic classes and imperfect to telic classes in production is a later development" (p. 245). Montrul and Perpiñán (2011) found that L2 learners were less likely to accept achievement predicates in the imperfect and stative verbs in the *pretérito*, and that these combinations are acquired later. Díaz et al. (2007), using a guided production task to elicit written data in which students were asked to complete three stories in the past, found a strong correlation between states with the Spanish *imperfecto* and achievements with the Spanish *pretérito simple*. Even if in generative accounts the nature of LAsp categories is read off the syntax whereas in cognitive-emergentist accounts it is formed bottom-up from the input, the suggestion for second language acquisition is identical. L2 learners likely come to the learning task equipped with a mental principle that enables them to scan the input in search of telic and atelic predicates. The difference between approaches is the following: generative scholars suggest that this mental principle precedes the input, while nongenerative scholars suggest that it is derived from the input.

2.5 The Discourse Account

When telling a story, native speakers of any language provide two kinds of information: foreground and background (Bardovi-Harlig, 2012). Hopper (1979) claims that events of foreground information are usually reported in temporal continuity (they follow a chronological order), are punctual (nondurative) and are completed (not ongoing). Background information likely concerns events that do not necessarily unfold alongside the story; that are likely durative, repetitive or habitual; and that are often ongoing. Let us repeat here sentence (1) from the Section 1 of this Element:

(1) *When Marco looked through the window, he saw Elena watching TV*

The predicates 'Marco looked through the window' and 'he saw Elena' provide foreground information. They move the story along. The reader/hearer can follow Marco while he is performing the two well-circumscribed actions. Instead, the predicate 'Elena watching TV' provides background information, something that can even be disconnected from the story, an event that the reader/hearer might perceive as preceding or unfolding in parallel with the actions carried out by Marco.

In L2 acquisition researchers found that a relationship exists between the learners' use of verbal morphology and the grounding of the narrative (von Stutterheim & Klein, 1989; Bardovi-Harlig, 1992). The discourse hypothesis (DH) predicts that "learners use emerging verbal morphology to distinguish foreground from background in narratives" (Bardovi-Harlig, 1994, p. 43) and that the foreground would be marked by the perfective past. The DH introduces a new factor in the study of the acquisition of the Tense-Aspect system. It is not just LAsp that might orient L2 learners toward the choice of the perfective or imperfective. The other factor at play is narrative grounding. Bardovi-Harlig (2012, p. 6) sums up the differences and the similarities between the two approaches:

> The DH predicts that all foregrounded predicates will attract perfective past. The LAH predicts telic predicates will receive perfective morphology, regardless of grounding, but the DH suggests that foreground telics are more likely too. The hypotheses make the same predictions for achievements and accomplishments in the foreground (they will attract the perfective past) and activities and states in the background (they are unlikely to attract the perfective), and they make different predictions for telic predicates in the background and atelic predicates in the foreground. In practicality, of the atelics only activities occur with frequency in both foreground and background. In the narratives of less proficient learners, activities clearly show perfective morphology only in the foreground, and in more proficient learners in background as well.

Mueller (2018) observed that the DH might not apply to all learners. In fact, this author observed that some proficient learners studied by Bardovi-Harlig (1992) seemed to be totally insensitive to discourse factors. Moreover, the DH "has not been expanded beyond narration to a full range of discourse contexts and thus would not apply to the tense-aspect asymmetry if sentences were not embedded in extended narrative" (p. 5).

2.6 The L1 Transfer Account

In its early formulation, the LAH could be considered a 'strong' hypothesis: its predictions were held to be universally valid, regardless of the language pairs or the learning context. Later, the strongest tenets of the LAH were modulated and factors other than prototypicality and frequency were taken into account. We now focus on the factor of L1 transfer.

It has been proposed that, especially in the early phases of acquisition, learners may project the aspectual (either LAsp or GA) values of L1 predicates onto L2 predicates. These values may or may not coincide, depending on the L1–L2 pairing (see Shirai, 2013, for a discussion). For example, L1 Spanish–L2 Italian learners will assume that *arrivare* 'arrive' and *cadere* 'fall' are telic because the corresponding verbs in Spanish (*llegar* and *caer*) are telic. Additionally, L1 Spanish–L2 Italian learners may be more accurate than L1 English learners in selecting the Italian perfective or the imperfective morphemes in the past because in Spanish the *pretérito perfecto simple* and the *imperfecto* share features with the Italian *passato prossimo* and *imperfetto*, respectively, while in English this aspectual distinction is blurred. A different view - which we do not examine here - is that positive transfer cannot always exert its influence because it is the complexity of the phenomenon, not L1–L2 differences, that determines whether and when acquisition occurs (e.g., Gabriele & McClure, 2011).

Studies that explore the effect of L1 transfer in the acquisition of L2 Aspect are quite numerous. For example, Izquierdo and Collins (2008) investigated how L1 Spanish and L1 English learners chose past tenses in L2 French. They found that English speakers made more mistakes because they chose the perfective as the default form, whereas Spanish learners relied on L1–L2 similarities and therefore made the relevant aspectual perfective–imperfective distinctions. McManus (2015), when comparing English and German learners of L2 French, also found that in progressive contexts, English learners outperformed German learners, probably because German lacks a progressive form.

In the studies discussed above, the L1 influence seems to play a role especially or exclusively at early and intermediate stages of acquisition. González and Quintana-Hernández (2018) used a written production task to compare two groups of L2 Spanish learners with Dutch and English L1s. They aimed to show that learners' use of GA was biased by particular aspectual features depending on their L1 grammatical realization of temporal and aspectual relations. The participants were asked to reconstruct a story from a muted short movie using past tenses. Results showed that English speakers overused the *pretérito* in both perfective and imperfective contexts. Dutch speakers instead used present perfect (*perfecto compuesto*) forms in perfective contexts and also the Imperfect. The fact that only the Dutch group used the present perfect for perfective contexts seems expected given that in Dutch there is a strong aspectual distinction between simple past and present perfect. Moreover, the fact that the English group blurred the aspectual distinction into a single past form seems to reinforce the L1 transfer hypothesis, because English does not distinguish between perfective and imperfective in the past. The authors concluded that "the L1 aspectual transfer is strong and shows differences which are predicted by the different grammatical representations of the three languages investigated in this experiment" (p. 12).

Diaubalick and Guijarro-Fuentes (2019) compared 30 L1 German learners with 30 L1 'Romance speakers' (L1 Italian, L1 French and L1 Portuguese), all learning L2 Spanish. Participants had to judge the acceptability of a sentence like (26):

(26) *Ayer me comía dos platos de paella, pero el segundo no me lo pude terminar*
Yesterday me eat.IMP two plates of paella, but the second not me it could.PRET finish
'Yesterday, I had two plates of paella, but I couldn't finish the second one'
(telic verb phrase in imperfective context)

The authors observed a sharp contrast between the German and the Romance groups in the acceptability of sentences and concluded that positive, similarity-based transfer from the L1 can accelerate acquisition.

Finally, it has been suggested that acquiring LAsp categories across language pairs might not be a symmetrical and balanced task. Acquiring Aspect can be more difficult in one language than in another. Shirai (2013, p. 276) reports that activity and achievement verbs are easy to distinguish in English but hard to distinguish in Japanese: "Different languages may bring about specific difficulties associated with particular distinctions" (p. 277). One might question whether the influence of the first language undermines the validity of the basic tenetes of the LAH. There are two opposing positions. One position holds that the influence of L1 transfer neither contradicts the tenets of the LAH nor undermines its universality (Tong & Shirai, 2016). Whether it is transferred from the native language or not, the telic–atelic divide would always guide the L2 acquisition of Aspect. The other position is that L1 transfer contradicts the assumption of universality and is incompatible with the presence of a cognitive drive that characterizes the original proposal of the LAH.

2.7 The Default Past Tense Hypothesis

The Default Past Tense Hypothesis (DPTH) makes three developmental predictions that significantly remodulate the tenets of the LAH and, even more importantly, introduce in the picture the factor of L2 proficiency. The first prediction of the DPTH is that initial learners will use just one default form to express all past meanings. This form is more likely to be the perfective than the imperfective because the latter is cognitively more complex, semantically more subtle and crosslinguistically less uniform and attested. The second prediction of the DPTH is that LAsp and discourse grounding increasingly affect past Tense marking as learners gain more experience with the target language. L2 learners constantly move toward prototypical associations as their knowledge of the language increases. It is worth recalling that the LAH predicts exactly the opposite: only initial associations will be prototypical in learner data. The third prediction of the DPTH is that the importance of LAsp is subordinate to the importance of discourse grounding because "grounding conveys a broader perspective than lexical aspect about the aspectual meaning of a text" (Salaberry, 2011, p. 184). Evidence confirming the DPTH comes from L1 English learners of Spanish who used a default perfective past marker in all contexts in Spanish, modelled on the use of the simple past in their native English Tense-Aspect system. Other evidence that prototypical associations 'go hand in hand' with L2 proficiency comes from L1 English learners of L2 French (McManus, 2013).

2.8 The Data and the Methods

The traditional, elective testing ground for the LAH was the analysis of corpus data, both cross-sectional and longitudinal. Housen (2000, p. 251) observed that "evidence for the correctness of the [L]AH must ultimately come from the observation of the predicted patterns of distribution and development of Tense-Aspect morphemes over time in L2 learner speech." In fact, in the last 30 years, the claims of the LAH were validated mainly through production tests of various kinds. The outcome variable in those data-driven analyses was whether or not learners' productions reflected the 'predicted patterns of distribution'. Given the variety of qualitative and quantitative approaches, it is normal, as underlined by Salaberry et al. (2013, p. 423), that so far "there has not been a systematic integration of findings across theoretical frameworks and methodological procedures." Among the early methods utilized, one can find especially narratives (personal and impersonal), description (of static and dynamic scenes) and conversation. Some tasks are more 'open-ended': for instance, free conversation, natural interaction and oral interviews where the topic was not predetermined. Others are instead constrained by more specific and codified elicitation procedures.

Among the constrained elicitation procedures, we first focus on oral and written film/story retells. Participants in these tests are usually shown a series of pictures (e.g., the 'Frog Story') or a brief clip (e.g., from Charlie Chaplin's *Modern Times*). They are then asked to retell what they have seen and are recorded while they do so. After transcribing and normalizing the recordings, researchers usually start by dividing the verb tokens by LAsp categories (the four Vendlerian classes) and by GA categories (e.g., the perfective and the imperfective past). In order to code verbs for LAsp categories, researchers sometimes – but not always – use aspectual diagnostics (Section 1.6). The result of this classification is usually a list of telic and atelic verbs and a list of perfective or imperfective verbs. Provided that the aspectual diagnostics utilized have worked well (e.g., that they give consistent results across native speaker raters), an important methodological problem arises: What should one do with these lists?

Let us assume that in our data three facts converge: (a) most perfectives uttered by learners are classifiable as telic (achievements and accomplishments) and most imperfectives atelic (states or activities); (b) the perfective-telic associations are sometimes overextended in contexts where the imperfective would be expected; and (c) the opposite never holds. Given these three conditions, can we conclude that our performance data confirm the predictions of the LAH? It probably depends on the criterion adopted for the count. Bardovi-Harlig (2002, p. 129) wrote that "the differences in these analyses could lead us to support or reject the [Lexical] Aspect Hypothesis on the basis of the very same data."

Calculating the across-category percentages (by counting, out of all perfective predicates, how many are telic or atelic) may be affected by the 'token bias'. This is the uneven distribution in the L1 input of perfective or imperfective predicates that may inflate or deflate their overall token count in learners' production. To counterbalance the token bias, Bardovi-Harlig (2002) proposed calculating the 'within-category percentages'. This is asking, for instance, out of all telic predicates in the sample, what percentage is inflected in the perfective and what percentage in the imperfective. The use of within-category percentages would neutralize the token bias because it immunizes the experimental sample against the natural imbalances in the number of perfective and imperfective tokens in the L1 input or requested by the kind of narrative (Bardovi-Harlig, 2002, p. 147).

Unfortunately, even this calculation cannot immunize against the risk that the sample is affected by another, underconsidered natural unbalance which is present in L1 input: the associative bias. As we will see (Section 3.3), it is not just the distribution of perfectives vs. imperfectives in the L1 input that is skewed, but the prototypical vs. nonprototypical lexeme–morpheme associations. Adult L2 learners are sensitive not only to raw token counts, but also, and above all, to contingency statistics (Wulf et al., 2009). For example, if an L2 Italian beginner learner is acquiring the past inflections of the telic predicate *cadere* 'fall' and if in the L1 input the perfective+telic association *è caduto* 'fell' is significantly more frequent than imperfective+telic *cadeva* 'was falling', then it is likely that this learner will implicitly record the skewed, contingent association between *cadere* and the perfective past morpheme. Every time the learner needs to express the meaning of *cadere*, she will use the perfective. This implies neither that the learner represents the perfective nor that she knows that *cadere* is telic. The count of perfective and imperfective occurrences of *cadere* in this learner's production might indicate their sensitivity to input distribution (contingency statistics) rather than the presence and effectiveness of the prototypicality principle in the learner's mind. In other words, one cannot know just from the fact that there are more perfectives with telic verbs whether learners associate telic verbs preferably with perfectives because the learner might be just mimicking the input. For this reason, one may disagree with Comajoan (2006) that "within-aspectual category percentages reflect the learner's competence rather than the input the learner receives, because the percentages treat all aspectual classes as equal regardless of the number of tokens in each aspectual category" (p. 225). As a matter of fact, not even LAsp classes 'are born equal' in the input: perfective and imperfective tokens attract, respectively, telic and atelic predicates in the L1 input, regardless of their absolute frequency, so that the impact on acquisition of input distribution and the prototypicality principle cannot be disentangled.

With respect to Housen's (2000, p. 251) observation reported above, it must be noted that within-learner analysis of longitudinal production data may be useful if one hopes to separate the influence of distribution in the L1 input from the cognitive developmental factors. For instance, experimental designs exist in which the same subjects are asked to retell the same story or film scene many times, at an interval of months spanning one year or so. In this case, significant within-subject variations in morpheme–lexeme associations are more likely to be attributable to a modification in a learner's aspectual competence rather than to the characteristics of L1 input alone (on the condition that one can establish that a learner's rate of exposure to L1 input remained constant).

Let us now turn to methods that focus on a learner's comprehension. One of the most-used methods is the interpretation task. Gabriele et al. (2003) tested learners on their interpretation of telic and atelic verbs in both perfective and imperfective past contexts. In the latter study, learners had to judge pairs of biclausal sentences like in (27) and (28):

(27) *My niece sang two Christmas songs at church. She left church after the first song*
(28) *My niece was singing two Christmas songs at church. She left church after the first song*

Learners had to decide whether or not the second clause presented a possible continuation of the first one. Results showed that learners properly rejected (27), but they also (unexpectedly) rejected (28). The latter result might indicate that L2 learners had difficulty assigning the correct interpretation to imperfective morphology in combination with a telic predicate ('she left church'). In Slabakova's (2000) experiment, participants were asked to assess on a scale from –3 to +3 how well two clauses in complex sentences, such as (29) and (30), combined with each other. The seven-point scale was used to give subjects sufficient space for encoding nuanced judgments between the two extremes: 'perfectly natural combination' and 'a very unnatural combination'.

(29) *Antonia worked in a bakery and made a cake*
(30) *Sharon worked in a bakery and made cakes*

Since the first clause in (29) is meant to establish a habitual situation, it is expected that the telic clause that follows (provided that participants know that the verb is telic; see Section 2.9.3) is considered a less-than-perfect match. On the other hand, the same habitual clause (30) in combination with an atelic second clause is expected to be judged as a better match than the one in (29).

The interpretation task can also be used in combination with pictures. Lee and Kim (2007) and Ryu et al. (2015) employed an interpretation task to test the acquisition of perfective and imperfective markers by L1 English and L1 Japanese learners of L2 Korean. The interpretation task included complete (perfective) and incomplete (progressive) items. Participants were asked to select the best-matching picture for the sentence. The three picture choices were made up of three distinct stages of an event: its inception, the action in progress and the resultant state after its completion. It was expected that pictures representing an action in progress would be matched with the progressive, whereas pictures representing the resultant states would be matched with the perfective.

These interpretation tasks target an L2 learner's capacity to consider GA and LAsp together – that is, to decide if the way the event is presented by verb morphology (as completed or ongoing) is compatible with the alleged presence or absence of an endpoint in the described situation. What the authors of these studies take for granted is that an L2 learner must know in advance if a given predicate is telic or atelic. This constitutes an instance of the 'comparative fallacy'.

2.9 Three Problems with the LAH

2.9.1 The LAH and the 'Comparative Fallacy'

Many studies supporting the LAH – in both the generative and usage-based approaches – take for granted that what seems to be a telic verb for the authors of the study is so in a learner's interlanguage as well. The point of this section stems from a question formulated in the title of Lakshmanan and Selinker (2001): How do we know what learners know? This question gave rise to a lively point–counterpoint debate in the following years (see Lardiere, 2003; Shirai, 2007). In their article, Lakshmanan and Selinker provided some reasons why the suppliance rate of a given form in an expected (mandatory) context alone should not be considered a valid criterion for evaluating L2 acquisition. They pointed out that the relationship between the emergence and use of an item (e.g., the inflectional morphology) on one side and the development of the representation of the corresponding abstract category (e.g., Tense or Aspect) on the other is not direct. In other words, what a learner produces does not necessarily coincide with what that learner meant to say, and the recoverability of the learner's intention "may be quite a difficult task to accomplish" (Lakshmanan & Selinker, 2001, p. 401). Lakshmanan and Selinker suggested that we needed more rigorous criteria if we want to avoid the comparative fallacy, which consists of superimposing target-like categories onto learner data (Bley-Vroman, 1983; Klein & Perdue, 1992). Reviewing the findings of an earlier work by Lardiere, Lakshmanan and Selinker (2001) suggested that verb semantics (LAsp) and discourse grounding distinctions are valid criteria for distinguishing genuine (non-target-like–oriented) obligatory contexts for past Tense markings because telic verbs and foreground events attract past perfective markings independently of the standpoint of the target language (overextensions).

In her reply to Lakshmanan and Selinker, Lardiere (2003) pointed out that investigating a learner's past Tense marking in relation to LAsp and discourse foregrounding is in fact at high risk of committing the comparative fallacy. Lardiere stated that "the [Lexical] Aspect Hypothesis studies appear to assume native speakers' intuitions about the meaning of verb stems in assigning coding categories such as activity, achievement, etc. to the data, and in applying diagnostic tests for those categories... these assumptions may indeed obscure our understanding of the L2 idiolect" (p. 136). Lardiere added that in SLA literature she could not find any discussion about whether the linguistic tests normally utilized to code data for L1 aspectual categories (operational, compatibility tests) were applicable to learner data (p. 138).

Shirai (2007), in his reply to Lardiere (2003), acknowledged that LAH studies might have assumed more semantic representations on the part of the learners than were warranted. He concluded that "in the analysis of production data, one should attempt maximum rigor in classification without reading in too much about learners' semantic representation" (p. 60). Shirai attempted to reduce the risk by taking into account the crosslinguistic variations of actionality. However, the problem does not arise from actional misclassification, but from taking for granted that L2 learners have clear and steady actional representations of the LAsp of the verbs they are using. How do we know, for example, that a verb that is classified as telic in the target language is also telic in a learner's interlanguage? This question remains largely unaddressed in the mainstream literature on the acquisition of L2 Aspect.

2.9.2 The LAH and the Lexicalist Bias

Most proponents of the LAH explicitly acknowledge that LAsp in both L1 and L2 is not a property of the lexical verb alone, but of its constellation (external and internal arguments and adjuncts). Many studies supporting the LAH report row scores and percentages of perfective/imperfective morphemes across LAsp categories and vice versa (see Section 2.3). As a matter of fact, in most of these studies, the LAsp categories taken as dependent variables are often represented by bare verbs, not by verb constellations. To make one example, when authors count up telic predicates, what they really count is often how many instances of 'jump', 'catch', 'ride into', 'run', etc., are in their data and how these verbs are inflected. Even though LAsp in theory is conceived compositionally, in practice it is mostly computed lexically. Yet, as we have seen, the context in which the verb appears can easily shift the verb's LAsp from one category to another. Salaberry and Martins (2014) report a convincing example of how this might occur. They quote two sentences from Slabakova and Montrul (2007) showing that the use of the Spanish *pretérito* is dependent on the animacy of the subject as shown by the contrast between the grammaticality of (31) and the agrammaticality of (32):

(31) *Roberto corrió (PRET) por la montaña*
O Roberto correu (PRET) ao longo da montanha
Roberto ran through the mountain

(32) *El río corrió (PRET) por la montaña
O rio correu ao longo da montanha
The river ran through the mountain

Salaberry and Martins (2014, p. 341) observe that, by modifying the context, one can turn (32) into an acceptable sentence in Spanish and Portuguese – for example, if one assumes that the bed of a river had been dry and that the gates of a dam were open to let the river run again. In such a case, they observe, it would be perfectly acceptable to use the Preterite.

Following this observation, Salaberry (2008) and Salaberry and Martins (2014) propose an important generalization: the more layers of plausible local contextual information one adds to the sentence, the more one will increase the possibility that also native speakers might disagree about the aspectual classification of a given verb occurring in that sentence. Importantly, even though

> this process is even more complex when we expand the range of interpretations to more than one language . . . in many cases, the analysis of data has been predicated on the analysis of sentences. . . . And, even in cases when learners are asked to generate language samples through narratives, video recalls and other open-ended productive tasks, the preponderance of the data can be regarded as decontextualized. (Salaberry and Martins, 2014, p. 342)

To sum up: Decontextualization represents an important methodological flaw in LAH research.

2.9.3 The LAH and the Lexical Underspecification of Early L2 Predicates

The analysis of learner corpora also suggests that (especially initial and low-intermediate) L2 learners' knowledge of the LAsp of L2 predicates should not be overinterpreted, for two reasons. First, learners – initial learners, especially – often overextend basic, frequent general purpose verbs where more specific verbs would be expected. Second, initial learners also often exchange verbs belonging to 'phasal pairs'. The word 'especially' here is important because the LAH makes predictions about early predicates.

As an example of the first phenomenon, L1 English beginner and intermediate learners of L2 Italian systematically use the basic, frequent verb of motion *andare* 'go' instead of *venire* 'come', although *venire* is telic and deictic, while *andare* is not. The basic verb *andare* is also used in L2 Italian instead of less frequent, more aspectually specified motion verbs such as *salire* 'get on', *arrivare* 'arrive', *avvicinarsi* 'get closer', *allontanarsi* 'move away', *raggiungere* 'reach', *volare* 'fly' (Rastelli, 2008, 2009; Rastelli & Vernice, 2013). Learners at initial and intermediate stages of acquisition interchange predicates with similar meanings but different LAs. For example, beginner and low-intermediate L1 Chinese–L2 Italian learners in an oral retelling task exchanged the atelic *guardare* 'look / watch' with *vedere* 'see', which, in its basic meaning of 'perceiving that something entered the visual field', is telic. These learners also often exchanged *sapere* and *conoscere*, both meaning 'know', and *dire* 'say' and *parlare* 'talk' (Giacalone Ramat & Rastelli, 2013).

The second phenomenon concerns 'phasal pairs'. Such pairs are made of verbs that can be seen as different phases of the same event (for the meaning of 'phase' in the event structure, see Moens & Steedman, 2005). For example, *cercare* 'look for' may serve as the preparatory phase of the event, while *trovare* 'to find' can serve as its culmination point. Comparable to phasal verbs (to some extent at least) are the reversive verbs (Cruse, 1997) such as *insegnare* 'teach' and *imparare* 'learn', *dare* 'give' and *ricevere* 'receive.' All these verbs are often exchanged by learners, regardless of their first language (Rastelli, 2008).

One can argue that these facts are only superficial, performance-related, or at most indicative of a developmental stage where poverty of vocabulary determines a learner's lexical and grammatical choices. This may be true, but the issue of overinterpretation of a learner's competence remains. Whatever the reasons for initial L2 learners to use one predicate while thinking of another, researchers are left with the dangerous choice between coding the LAsp of L2 predicates for their intended meaning or for their actual meaning. If a learner wrote *andare* 'go' but clearly meant *venire* 'come', should one label the predicate as telic or atelic? This methodological choice strongly affects the data that can be interpreted as supporting or disconfirming the LAH.

In Section 3, a deeper account of these facts will be provided. According to this interpretation, the data described above, taken together might indicate the presence of a temporary defective aspectual competence (Section 3.5). L2 learners at this stage might initially ignore or disregard whether the predicates of the target language are telic or atelic, because, as the whole Tense-Aspect system is in reconstruction, LAsp of the second language too is learned. If so, LAsp cannot pave the way for the acquisition of the Tense-Aspect system, as the LAH claims.

3 What Are the New Avenues for Research?

3.1 Moving Away from Traditional Data

Neurolinguistic and psycholinguistic techniques have gradually become the standard in the study of language. SLA research is not an exception to this trend. Studies concerning the relationship between language-related behaviors and the hidden signatures of the L2 learning brain have multiplied exponentially in the last ten years (for a recent review, see the special issue of *Second Language Research* vol. 34/1, 2018). Compared to the sophistication of those studies, the data on L2 acquisition of Aspect (from both production and comprehension tests) described in Section 2 – albeit fundamental and pioneering – appear now insufficient. Above all, traditional data cannot disentangle learners' representations from learners' processing. L2 learners might have clear aspectual representations of L2 aspectual categories and still be incapable of using such representations in real time. Or, on the other hand, learners might just be imitating the most frequent lexeme–morpheme combinations they've encountered in the input and using the expected form–function aspectual pairings as memory-based chunks, although the corresponding aspectual representations are not yet in place. While one may feel the need to move away from traditional research methods in general, in the specific domain of L2 Aspect, scholars need to abstract away especially from the count of prototypical and nonprototypical associations in learner data, whether they are calculated across-categories or within-categories. Even if percentages demonstrate that a given telic verb is used more frequently at the perfective than at the imperfective, we might still ignore whether or not a learner's competence incorporates the mental, abstract notions of 'telic' and 'perfective'. As noticed also by Roberts and Liszka (2013, p. 418), moving away from the count of perfective-telic and imperfective–atelic associations is a prerequisite for researchers studying interlanguage. Learners who can produce target-like prototypical pairings may yet have to acquire the underlying semantics of Tense-Aspect morphology. If one wants to analyze GA and LAsp from an interlanguage standpoint (minimizing the risk of committing the comparative fallacy), the preliminary concern should be how it is possible to tap into a learner's competence without taking for granted categories, such as LAsp, whose acquisition must be still proven.

3.2 Processing Studies on L2 Aspect

L2 processing studies analyze the time course and the hierarchical sequence of the cognitive operations that learners must activate in order to comprehend sentences. The combined analysis of reaction times (RT) and covariates (the whole set of learner-related or item-related independent, explanatory variables) is believed to open a window onto the mental architecture of the learner's grammatical representations (for a review of methods using RTs in SLA, see Gass et al., 2013, p. 61). Unfortunately, processing studies on Aspect are still extremely rare. In this section, we review four recent studies that utilized RTs (in combination with behavioral techniques) to investigate L2 learners' aspectual representations. At the end of the section, we will briefly comment upon what these studies share.

Roberts and Liszka (2013) questioned whether the aspectual knowledge that learners display in performance data can be applied automatically in real-time comprehension. The authors investigated whether L1 French and L1 German learners of L2 English were sensitive to mismatches in agreement between fronted temporal adverbials (e.g., 'Initially'/ 'Since last week') and the Tense/ Aspect of immediately following verbs ('ate'/ 'has eaten'), as shown in sentence (33), in their online comprehension of the target language:

(33) a. *Initially, the cat ate/*has eaten only fish*
b. *Since last week, the cat *ate/has eaten only fish*

As we have seen, the English present perfect can be used with reference to the present (since it includes the TU) but not with an adverbial specifying definite past (which excludes the TU). Twenty German and 20 French adult advanced learners of L2 English participated in the experiment. Importantly, all participants were able to distinguish the past simple from the present perfect in an offline cloze test prior to the experiment. The experiment comprised two tasks: an offline acceptability judgment task measuring explicit knowledge, and a self-paced reading experiment to tap into implicit knowledge. In the self-paced reading task, the participants saw sentences like (33) presented word by word. The participant used a push-button box to bring up the first word of the sentence, and then continued to push the button on the box to bring up each subsequent word, which replaced the former in the center of the screen. Delays in pushing the button indicate difficulties in the processing of the previous 'region of interest' (the fragment of the sentence).

Results showed that in the offline experiment all groups (the L2 learners and the native speaker controls) found the match conditions more acceptable than the mismatch conditions, as was expected. However, results from the self-paced reading task showed that, with items in the past simple, only the L1 French participants showed a processing cost (a delay in pushing the button) in the mismatch condition in their online reading times. With items at the present perfect, the mismatch conditions elicited longer reading times than the match conditions for both the native English and the L1 French participants, but not for the L1 German participants. The authors commented on the results as follows:

> the judgment task showed that all three groups found the mismatch conditions less acceptable than the match conditions. Thus all participants demonstrated their explicit knowledge of the English past simple and present perfect. Despite this, the two L2 groups patterned differently from each other in their online processing of the experimental sentences. The French L2 learners' processing reflected their off-line, metalinguistic judgments: they found

> the mismatch conditions more difficult to process than the match conditions of both the past simple and the present perfect items. In contrast, the German L2 learners did not show a processing cost for either the past simple or the present perfect mismatch items. (Roberts & Liszka, 2013, p. 427)

The authors suggested that "French learners could be more susceptible to the salience of Aspect in English in general, as French also overtly marks Aspect, creating a heightened sensitivity in these learners" (p. 429).

Roberts and Liszka (2019) used self-paced reading to investigate whether a learner's knowledge of aspectual differences (the contrast between past simple/progressive) of a previously encountered English verb in the first part of a garden-path sentence[5] (e.g., 'played') affects learners' subsequent processing of the potential direct object (e.g., 'the song'), like in sentence (34):

(34) *While the band played the song pleased all the customers*

The authors wanted to test whether L2 English learners' reading of temporarily ambiguous sentences showed their sensitivity to the distinction between [+/– progressive] Aspect, which in English is blurred in the past. If an L2 learner automatically incorporates the aspectual knowledge that 'played' can be progressive, then, depending on the context, we expect that their interpretation of the sentences will or will not be disrupted when they encounter the direct NP 'the song'. The authors also used self-paced readings to tap into implicit processes and acceptability judgments to assess explicit knowledge. Participants were 32 L1 German, 24 L1 Dutch and 24 L1 French advanced L2 English learners and a control group of 20 native (British) English speakers. The results showed that all learners performed like native speakers in their processing/interpretation of the past simple items. In fact, all participants slowed down (indicating an attempt to reinterpret the sentence) immediately after they read 'rabbit':

(35) *As John hunted the frightened rabbit escaped through the dark trees*

This online pattern was reflected in all the learners' offline judgments as well. However, the three learner groups behaved differently with the progressive, as in sentence (36):

(36) *As John was hunting the frightened rabbit escaped through the dark trees*

The German learners – despite demonstrating metalinguistic knowledge of the distinction between the progressive and the simple in the acceptability

[5] In a garden-path sentence, readers are lured towards a given interpretation until they encounter an element that forces them to revise such interpretation and reparse the sentence from scratch.

judgments task – showed the same preference/expectations for the direct object ('the frightened rabbit') without distinguishing between the simple past and the progressive. Highly proficient L1 French learners, on the other hand, performed most similarly to the English natives and took into account the atelic reading of 'as John was hunting' (not necessarily requiring an object), although the French *imparfait* differs from the English past progressive in that it can express both ongoing and habitual events in the past. Finally, the Dutch group performed similarly to the French on the offline task, showing an effect of their knowledge of aspectual (± progressive) distinction in English, whereas in the online task no such effects were observed (Roberts and Liszka, 2019, p. 20). The authors argued that that L2 processing and offline interpretations of aspectual distinction in this study were influenced by whether or not a learner's L1 encodes progressive Aspect via syntactic (French) or only lexical means (German) (see Sections 1.9; 2.4).

Vogel (2017) reported findings from 3 language tasks with 98 L1 English subjects learning L2 Spanish (30 intermediate and 33 advanced) and 35 native Spanish speakers. The purpose of the study was to compare native and nonnative comprehension of Spanish aspectual contrasts. First, two offline cloze tasks (a story-in-context cloze task and an isolated sentence cloze task) were utilized to measure the participants' knowledge of perfective and imperfective Aspect. In the first one, the participants had to choose the correct verb from two possible past Tense verb forms: one perfective, the other imperfective. The first two lines of the cloze task are reported in (37):

(37) _________ *(Había, hubo) una vez tres osos que* _________ *(vivían, vivieron) en el*
bosque: papá oso, mamá osa y el pequeño osito. Un día mamá osa _________ *(hacía, hizo)*
una sopa de arroz con pollo y _________ *(ponía, puso) tres platos en la mesa*

'Once upon a time there lived three bears in the forest: papa bear, mama bear, and little bear. One day mama bear made a rice and chicken soup and put three plates on the table'

The forced binary choice sentence-picture matching task had three steps. First, the participants read a sentence (like 38a or 38b below) that contained either the perfective or the imperfective. Then, participants were presented with two pictures representing a completed event and an ongoing event.

(38) a. *El hombre tocó el piano*
'The man played the piano'

b. *El hombre tocaba el piano*
'The man was playing the piano'

Finally, the participants had to decide which picture best represented the sentence that they read in the first step. Unlike the cloze test, the forced choice test was timed. Immediately after reading the sentence, the participants had to press the spacebar on the keyboard. As the participant pressed the spacebar, the sentence disappeared from the screen and the two pictures appeared side by side. Participants had to press the key corresponding to their choice. This task generated data on both the participants' accuracy rates and their reaction times.

In the self-paced reading task, participants were asked to determine whether or not the sentence they read was logical. All sample sentences consisted of coordinated clauses conjoined by a conjunctional phrase. Some of the combinations made sense, while others were contradictory.

Before presenting the results of the three tests, Vogel (2017) importantly acknowledged that "whereas offline tasks have no time limit and allow the participants to think about the meaning of the sentence and potentially access metalinguistic information before making a decision, online comprehension tasks allow less time for metalinguistic abilities to be engaged." To support this important point, the author quoted VanPatten et al. (2012, p. 118): "the advantage of on-line methods in L2 research is that they avoid the potential introspection and resultant tapping of explicit knowledge that can come from paper-and-pencil tests." On the offline cloze test, the native Spanish speakers outperformed the L2 learners, and the advanced L2 learners outperformed the intermediate L2 learners. Therefore, Spanish proficiency clearly affected choice of Aspect on these two offline tasks in terms of accuracy. The author suggested that L2 learners were able to distinguish between aspectual distinctions, possibly drawing upon metalinguistic knowledge gained via explicit instruction. In the sentence-picture matching task, all three learner groups performed most accurately on perfective accomplishments, most quickly on imperfective activities and least quickly on imperfective accomplishments. According to the author, this supports the predictions of the LAH – namely, that accomplishments are applied to the perfective Aspect early in development.

The results from the self-paced reading task were rather surprising, for two reasons. First, L2 learners, in general, did not correctly interpret the meanings of the experimental sentences. The intermediate L2 learners scored 51 percent overall on both sentence types, and the advanced L2 learners scored 56 percent. Second, L2 learners slowed down at the regions of interest, especially at the verb region, for both logical and illogical sentences. The author interpreted such results as a cue for processing difficulty. In fact, L2 learners were slower and less accurate than L1 Spanish speakers at processing both logical and illogical sentences. This means that although explicit knowledge of the Spanish perfective–imperfective contrast might have been in place, possibly via classroom instruction, learners could not make use of this knowledge in real-time processing.

Rastelli (2019) studied the 'imperfective paradox' in a second language with a dynamic completion-entailment test. The imperfective paradox (IP) refers to the fact that the imperfective-progressive yields completion entailment with atelic predicates (e.g., Livia was pushing the chair → Livia pushed the chair = true) but not with telic predicates (Livia was peeling the tangerine → Livia peeled the tangerine = not necessarily true). The research question concerned whether L2 learners, like adult native speakers, were sensitive to the IP. Native speakers of Italian are sensitive to the IP for three reasons: (a) they distinguish between perfectives and imperfectives; (b) they distinguish between telic and atelic predicates (the IP works only for the former); and (c) they can disentangle GA and LAsp. Therefore, through the lens of the IP, the study investigated the presence of all these features simultaneously in an adult L2 Italian learner's aspectual competence.

A novel technique – the Interval-Based Truth-Value (IBT) judgment test – was utilized in this study. In the IBT, participants watched a short video clip and interrupted it by pushing a button as soon as they judged that the person in the video ('Livia') had carried out the action described by the displayed sentence. In this task, implicit timed interruptive clicks substituted for participants' explicit yes/no decisions about the completion entailment elicited by sentences used in traditional completion test (e.g., *If you stop in the middle of V-ing, have you V-ed?*). The task wording in the IBT was as follows:

> In this simulation game, you are a teacher of Italian administering an official exam. Livia has been preparing to take this exam for months and now it's her turn. The system will sort out and display on the screen a sentence in Italian. In order to demonstrate that her Italian has really improved, Livia must simulate exactly what is written in the sentence. As the fair and impartial examiner you must be, push the button to interrupt the clip as soon as you think that Livia has done exactly what is written in the sentence.

Each video clip comprised four phases, representing the temporal ontology of events proposed by Moens and Steedman (2005), which corresponded to the lexical Aspect features of [±inchoative], [±activity] and [±telic]. Figure 2 visualizes how the event corresponding to the perfective sentence Livia ha spinto la sedia 'Livia pushed/has pushed the chair' flows across the phases of

Figure 2 The event-flow across four phases (the preparation phase has been excluded here): start, duration, culmination and resulting state. The labels in the frames were not shown to participants.

(i) preparation and start (Livia grabs the chair), (ii) duration (Livia pushes it across a room), (iii) culmination (Livia arrives at a desk and stops), and (iv) resulting state (Livia sits on the chair):

Ninety-nine nonnative speaker (NNS) L1 Chinese, L1 Russian and L1 Spanish participants with various proficiencies took part in the experiment. A total of 32 experimental sentences were derived from 8 telic (accomplishment) and 8 atelic (activity) predicate-events. Each predicate occurred once in the perfective and once in the imperfective-progressive (e.g., *Livia ha spinto/spingeva la sedia* 'Livia pushed the chair'; *Livia ha sbucciato/sbucciava il mandarino* 'Livia peeled the tangerine'). Predicates were coded as telic or atelic by an independent sample of 107 Italian NSs.

The first important result was that, in the presence of perfective-telic events, NSs and, to a limited extent, more advanced learners (especially L1 Spanish speakers) tended to click toward the final phases of the event, whereas beginner and intermediate NNSs interrupted video clips for perfective and imperfective telic predicates at similar phases. This suggests that most L2 learners were not sensitive to the effects of the shift in ±perfective morphology on sentence interpretation. The second result is even more striking. Only NSs and, to a limited extent, more advanced NNSs (especially L1 Spanish speakers) waited for the final (culmination or result) phases before interrupting telic (but not atelic) perfectives. This indicates that most learners were not capable of distinguishing between telic and atelic predicates in the target language – that is, initial and intermediate L2 learners, unlike NSs, could not recognize the culmination point that characterizes perfective-telic predicates (which can be considered complete only when the culmination point is reached). We will return to this crucial point at the end of this section.

The studies by Roberts and Liszka (2013, 2019) and Vogel (2017) share a stark contrast between offline and online results. Whereas the former measures seem to confirm the LAH, the latter seem not to. This contrast might be interpreted in two ways: (a) L2 learners who already possess clear representations of L2 aspectual distinctions cannot use such representations in real-time processing; and (b) offline measures – production data included – cannot tap into a learner's aspectual competence: they can, at most, tap into explicit knowledge. The results from Rastelli (2019) fit explanation (b) and cast doubt on the basic tenets of the LAH (Section 3.5).

3.3 Statistical studies on the acquisition of L2 aspect

The distributional account of the LAH (Section 2.3) contends that early perfective predicates are learned because the frequency of telic-perfective predicates in the input, together with the prototypicality principle, prompts learners to induce and abstract away the function(s) of the perfective morpheme. Actually, the percentages of prototypical telic-perfective predicates might not be indicative enough. Research on statistical learning has pointed out that the impact of raw frequency on L1 and L2 acquisition has been overrated (Baayen, 2010). Items that are less frequent could be acquired earlier, more easily and more stably than more frequent items, provided that the former co-occur with an above-average frequency in patterns of associations with other items. Said differently, it is not just the raw frequency in the input that makes acquisition easier; rather, it is the probability that two items, or a lexical item and a construction – e.g., a verb lexeme and the perfective – attract each other and co-occur much more frequently than would normally be expected given their frequencies in isolation. This shift toward the study of item associations marked a revolution in statistical learning research. In spite of this, much corpus linguistic work in SLA still underutilizes the probabilistic information corpora may offer, "limiting itself to comparing absolute and relative frequencies of types and tokens" (Gries, 2018, p. 734). Actually, in the last decade various measures of association/contingency started to attract the interest also of SLA scholars (e.g., Ellis, 2016). The idea that L2 learners are sensitive especially to exceptional co-occurrence of lexemes and constructions in the input became increasingly popular. According to usage-based approaches, grammatical constructions – such as perfectives – 'have a meaning' because speakers tend to associate them more frequently and stably with some lexical items – e.g., specific classes of verbs – rather than with others. We have seen (Section 2.8) that L2 learners' sensitivity to lexeme-construction contingency could trigger the acquisition of abstract grammatical categories, such as Aspect.

A few studies have investigated how the various exponents of association/contingency in the L1 input may impact L2 acquisition. Wulff et al. (2009) focused on two native corpora: the spoken section of the British National Corpus (BNC, 10 million words) and the Michigan Corpus of Academic English (MICASE, 1.7 million words). In order to code the telicity of L1 predicates, 20 native speakers of American English were presented with a questionnaire with verbs in isolation, without arguments and in their base form. Subjects were instructed to evaluate each verb with regard to how strongly it implies an endpoint expressed in values from 1 (if there is no endpoint implied) to 7 (if an endpoint is strongly implied). Three examples were given: 'smash' as a highly telic verb, 'continue' as highly atelic and 'swim' as somewhere in between. The resulting telicity rating data demonstrated that those verbs distinctly associated with the past Tense in the input received significantly higher telicity ratings than verbs associated with the progressive (Wulff et al. 2009, p. 103). The authors then compared telicity ratings and the lexeme–morpheme association scores extracted from learner corpora. Using multiple distinctive collexeme analysis (Gries & Stefanowitsch, 2004) and unidirectional contingency-based measure delta-p ΔP, they found that the verbs that emerged first (and were learned first) in the progressive were also highly atelic and frequent in and distinctly associated with the progressive in the input. Likewise, the verbs first learned in the past Tense were highly telic and frequent in and distinctly associated with the past Tense (p. 104). Tracy-Ventura and Cuesta Medina (2018) found an identical distributional bias in L1 Spanish, with several telic predicates more often occurring in the *pretérito* and several atelic predicates in the *imperfecto*. The study of association scores concerned various kinds of constructions, not only Aspect. Ellis and Ferreira-Junior (2009) investigated how L1 distribution could influence L2 acquisition of the verb locative, verb object locative and ditransitive constructions. They also found that first-learned verbs were not only highly frequent for their respective constructions, but were also strongly attracted to and prototypical of them.

The aforementioned statistical studies on Aspect do not deal directly with two important issues. First, as Tracy-Ventura and Cuesta Medina (2018) acknowledged, corpus data might not reflect the input addressed to learners. Second, the problem of the causal relationship between frequency and prototypicality (Section 2.2) remains unaddressed also in studies based on association scores. Wulff et al. (2009, p. 355) suggested that the greater the token frequency of an exemplar, the more likely it will be considered prototypical by L2 learners. For example, the telic predicates most strongly associated with the perfective are expected to be among the most frequent perfectives in the input. Actually, this is not always the case; the Italian verb *andare* 'go' is a clear counterexample. In fact, *andare* 'go' at the perfective (*andato*) is by far the most frequent motion verb in both L1 and L2 Italian, despite its LAsp being totally underspecified (e.g., in the sentence *il motore va* 'the engine is working', *andare* it is atelic, whereas in the sentence *vado a casa* '(I) go home' *andare* it is telic). In this and many other cases, frequency and prototypicality radically diverge in the L1 input and L2 production data. This particularly holds true in the presence of general-purpose predicates or 'light verbs' (such as 'do', 'make', 'get', 'go', 'say', 'see'), which are both very frequent in the input and also aspectually underspecified (Rastelli, 2020).

3.4 What is Still Missing? Data from Event-related Potentials

Research on the brain signatures of Aspect of (typical and atypical developing) adults, children and even infants have used electrophysiological data (event-related potentials [ERP]) and functional magnetic resonance imaging (fMRI) for at least 12 years (e.g., Baggio et al., 2008; Romagno et al., 2012; Malaia et al., 2009; Pace et al., 2020). It is therefore understandable that in 2006, Slabakova (2006)[6] could find no ERP study on the acquisition of L2 Aspect (although L2 studies using ERP had been published since 1996). Unfortunately, the situation has not changed since then. To my knowledge, electrophysiological and neuroimaging studies on L2 Aspect using ERP and fMRI are still missing, yet they would be greeted by many as a much-needed change of perspective in the field. ERP data would be particularly revealing about L2 learners' developing aspectual representations. They would tell us not only what learners can do, but possibly also what they really *know* about what they are doing.

ERPs measure electrical activity at the cortex. In ERP experiments, electrodes are placed on the participant's scalp. Participants then read or listen to sentences one word at a time on a screen. Usually these sentences contain semantic or grammatical (morphosyntactic, categorical) anomalies. When the critical word or region is read or heard, neurons in the cortex – which share depth, form and orientation of axons – co-activate ('fire together') to cope with the comprehension problem. This activation alters the brain's surface electricity because of the passage of ions (the chemical signal) from the axons of the efferent neuron to the dendrite spines of the afferent one. Researchers record,

[6] "Semantic structure is violated, also, when we combine an inherently telic predicate (the achievement recognize) with for X time adverbial which is felicitous with atelic predicates . . . To my knowledge, the inquiry into early vs. late bilingualism is still awaiting neurolinguistic studies using this type of linguistic stimuli" (Slabakova, 2006, p. 315).

amplify and clean the electrical signal of noise, then overlap all sentences in the same experimental condition and across all participants. In particular, they compare sentences in the grammatical vs. ungrammatical conditions. By doing so, they often notice that different anomalies consistently elicit different brain responses – that is, waveforms having different polarity (positive or negative), amplitude (duration), latency (after the onset of the critical word) and distribution on the scalp. These different waves reflecting changes in brain electricity (in terms of microvolts) are called 'components'.

Three components are well-known in language studies. Lexical-semantic anomalies (like in the famous sentence 'he spread his warm bread with socks') or infrequent, unexpected words or combinations of words elicit a negative wave between 300 and 500 ms after the onset of the critical word. This component is called N400. On the contrary, in the presence of morphosyntactic and categorial anomalies (but also at post-processing revision stages and due to wrap-up effects) – such as in a sentence like 'The children plays in the garden' – the brain elicits the LAN (Left Anterior Negativity) and the P600 components between 300–500 ms and 600 ms after the onset of the critical word, respectively. Many (but not all) longitudinal ERP studies in SLA indicate that P600 and especially LAN could be the markers or native-like attainment of L2 morphosyntax. Only proficient learners would respond to a morphosyntactic violation with P600 (much more rarely preceded by a LAN). Nonproficient learners would instead respond to a morphosyntactic violation with an N400. This means that less-proficient learners would treat morphosyntactic violations just as infrequent ('never heard before') words or an infrequent combination of words. As learners' proficiency increases, a shift would be expected from an N400 to a P600 for the same violation (e.g., Osterhout et al., 2006). This would be a marker of attainment of L2 morphosyntax. This pattern has been observed in at least a dozen studies, to the extent that a standard assumption nowadays in SLA is that the presence of P600 (with or without LAN) is a marker of native-like grammatical processing, while N400 is a marker of lexical statistical processing of L2 morphosyntax (Morgan-Short & Ullman, 2011).

Let us now return to the utility of ERP studies for L2 Aspect research. Let us recall one big unresolved (and unaddressed) issue in the study of L2 Aspect: do L2 learners use the expected telic-perfective association because they represent telicity and perfectivity in their minds (either as values to be filled in a functional head or as cognitive universal operating principles), or because they are just mimicking a statistical tendency in the input? Let us imagine that a novice L2 English learner reads or listen to pairs (39a) and (39b), the former containing a violation – that is, an adverbial expression that is incompatible with a telic predicate (Slabakova, 2006, p. 315):

(39) a. **John recognized the man in the picture for an hour*
b. *John recognized the man in the picture in an hour*

If the analysis of ERP components does not reveal any difference in the learner's processing of (39a–b), then we might be in the position to argue that the L2 English learner is not (yet) sensitive to an important consequence of the telic–atelic distinction in the target language, which is the (in)compatibility with punctual adverbs. If a learner ignores an important consequence of telicity, how could one maintain that the learner knows that an L2 predicate such as 'recognize' is telic or atelic? We could go even further. If an initial learner does not know whether an L2 predicate is telic or atelic, how can one maintain that telicity paves the way for the acquisition of Tense-Aspect morphology? Let us then imagine that the same sentence (39a) over a certain period of time in the same learner elicits an N400 exactly after the region 'for an hour'. At this point we might argue that the learner's aspectual competence is developing. In fact, that learner likely perceived an anomaly in the sentence and the anomaly was likely triggered by the adverbial. Finally, let us suppose that after some more time – say, four months – the same violation elicits a P600 component. Then we can advance the hypothesis that the learner might have identified the source of the anomaly at a higher (sentence) level, probably in the combination between the form of the verb, the adverbial expression, the kind of object NP ('the man in the picture'), etc. This is because the P600 is often a cue of sentence reanalysis or 'wrap-up'.

3.5 What If LAsp Too is Learned?

The prototype account explains why speakers and learners are predisposed to associate telic predicates and perfective morphology and, as a consequence, why such associations are so frequent in the input (Section 2.2). The distributional account explains how such telic-perfective prototypical associations are learned from the input (Section 2.3). The LAH took it a step further by combining those two accounts and predicting that, since prototypical associations are both more natural and more frequent, L2 learners will acquire them first. However, this step is not logically necessary; it is in fact a stipulation. In SLA, there are many instances of allegedly more 'natural' and 'intuitive' (always so from the target-language standpoint) and more frequent (and/or frequently associated) features that, contrary to any prediction, resist acquisition: for example, clitic pronouns, case (e.g., the distinction between 'I' and 'me' in English), number and gender agreement, auxiliaries 'be' and 'have', and many others. Studies exist that – without denying the role of frequency and prototypicality – cast doubt at least on the strongest version of the developmental predictions of the LAH (e.g., Dietrich et al., 1995; Giacalone, 1995; Huang,

2008; Salaberry, 2011; McManus, 2013; Rastelli & Vernice, 2013; Rastelli, 2019). This is true to such an extent that Yasuhiro Shirai – one of the main proponents of the LAH – recently put forth the 'Lexical Insensitivity Hypothesis', which claims that beginner L2 learners are insensitive to LAsp. As proficiency improves, learners become more sensitive and produce Tense-Aspect markers in a way more restricted by the predicates' actional templates (Tong & Shirai, 2016, p. 20). However, if aspectual competence only emerges late, how can initial L2 learners know whether a verb is telic or not? This question, again, does not target the descriptive adequacy of the LAH, but its explanatory adequacy (Section 4.1), and it can be rephrased as: where does an initial L2 learner's knowledge of aspectual distinctions come from? If these distinctions are innate, then they take a lot of time to be instantiated, and divergent, unexpected data from initial and intermediate learners must be explained. If they come only from the input and learners are just mimicking, then selective overextensions must be explained. Finally, if aspectual representations come mainly or exclusively from a learner's L1, then any assumption of universality in the LAH is lost.

Some years ago, an alternative hypothesis was advanced (Rastelli, 2008, 2009, 2019; Rastelli & Vernice, 2013). A developmental pattern could instead exist which constrains the ways learners can represent the LAsp of L2 predicates over time, regardless of their L1s. L2 learners, unlike NSs, may initially ignore telicity because LAsp too is learned, that is, is in reconstruction. The learning algorithm of LAsp would stipulate that in a beginner-to-intermediate learner's competence, the telic vs. atelic distinction of L2 predicates is underspecified. In the meantime, learners focus on features of the verb meaning other than LAsp. As their proficiency increases, learners would gradually learn to recognize the features distinguishing telic from atelic predicates.

The developmental stages of the reconstruction of LAsp categories in an L2 are still unexplored. Nevertheless, at least three cues of its existence have been identified in early interlanguages of L2 Italian learners. These cues are (a) the use of the perfective morpheme to confer a telic interpretation on underspecified verbs; (b) the use of adjuncts (adverbs and prepositions) to indicate a culmination point overtly; and (c) the overuse of so-called 'basic verbs' (Viberg, 2002) in place of more lexically specified verbs. All such cues have been found in prompted written narratives by L1 Chinese and L1 English learners of L2 Italian. For example, in one prompted narrative experiment (Rastelli & Vernice, 2013), 143 undergraduate American students spending one semester of their second or third university year on a study-abroad program in Italy were asked to describe a short clip in which two telic events overlap. In the scene used as the stimulus, a woman exits a restaurant (event A) and sees her bus with her travel-mates leaving without her (event B). The ordered sequence is visualized in Figure 3.

Figure 3 The ordered sequence of frames from the clip used as stimuli. Frames 1 and 2 refer to event A, frames 3 and 4 refer to event B.

The authors reported that, while most NSs chose the telic verb *uscire* 'exit' at the present Tense to describe event A – like in sentence (40) – about 80 percent of beginner students used the periphrasis *andare fuori* 'go out' at the past perfective, like in sentence (41):

(40) *Quando lei esce vede che il suo pullman parte*
'when she exits (she) sees that her bus is leaving'

(41) *Quando lei è andata fuori il suo autobus già parte*
'When she has gone outside, her bus has already left'

In terms of event structure (Pustejovsky, 1991), both *uscire* and *andare fuori* can be 'transition verbs', but only *uscire* 'exit' has an interpretive focus on the resulting state depending on the presence of a resultative predicate 'be-at (x,y)' in its logical structure (Dowty, 1979; van Valin, 1990). In contrast, *andare fuori* 'go out' is commonly used to express the direction of motion and not necessarily the attainment of the final state of 'being outside'. In sentence (41), beginner learners especially seem to utilize two simultaneous strategies to describe the woman's state of being outside. To account for such strategies, we adapted the representation of inner Aspect couched within the VP shells, as proposed by Travis (2010). First, unlike NSs, learners might not distinguish between GA and LAsp (e.g., between outer and inner Aspect, in Verkuyl's 1993 terms). In this

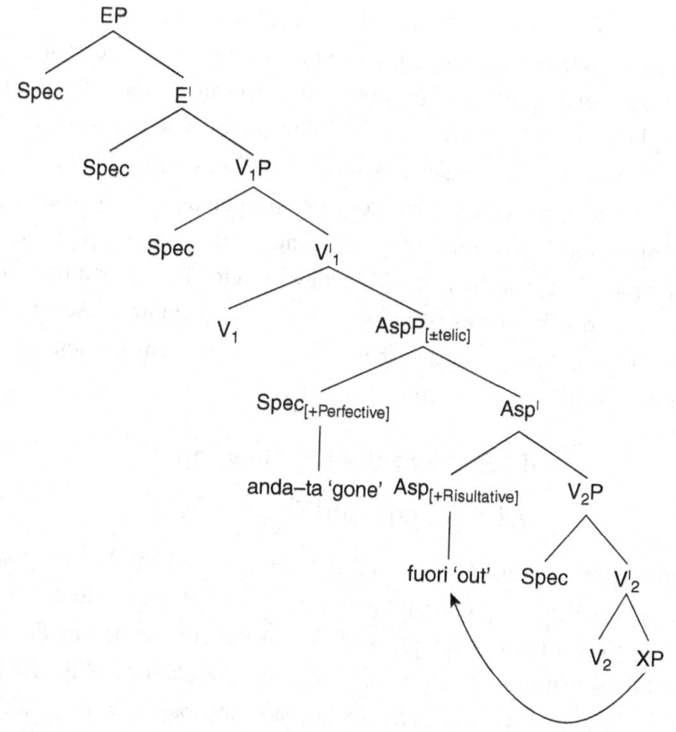

Figure 4 Syntactic configuration of the telic interpretation of the predicate *andata fuori* 'gone out' in sentence (36) (adapted from Travis, 2010).

case, the past morphology of *andata fuori* 'gone outside' would be used to express not only the boundedness of the event (pertaining to GA) but also the presence of a culmination point in the motion event (which pertains to LAsp). In the syntactic tree (Figure 4), the telic interpretation of *andata fuori* can be derived because the inflectional past perfective morpheme *-ta* of *andata* 'gone' is checked (and interpreted) at AspP – between the VP shells – rather than set apart in the GA domain (which would be above the Event Phrase, in the inflectional domain not visible in the syntactic tree in Figure 4).

As the second building block of a telic interpretation of *andata fuori*, learners might have upgraded the lowest XP complement (AdvP, but also PP) expressing the goal of motion (*fuori* 'outside') to the rank of external arguments at the AspP Spec position. The projection AspP may host raised PPs and AdvPs to signal that the resulting phase of the event *andare fuori* is the relevant dimension for its correct interpretation, although this resulting phase (or culmination point) is not a part of the logical structure 'be-at (x,y)' of V.

In conclusion, the hypothesis that LAsp in a second language is learned opens new and promising directions of research, but it also raises two preliminary questions. The first concerns the nature of learners' defective aspectual knowledgc and the counterintuitive idea that predicates – at least for a certain period – can be comprehended and used for their general meaning, regardless of LAsp. For example, in an initial learner's competence, one could expect that a single predicate expressing motion such as *andare* 'go' covers all kinds of motion events (directed, undirected, manner of motions, deictic, etc.); one single verb of perceiving with sight could cover 'see', 'watch' and 'observe'; the distinction between 'talk', 'tell' and 'say' could be blurred, etc. The second unaddressed question concerns the stages of reconstructing LAsp. Future research should focus on the existence of means that learners at different proficiency levels could use systematically to express (a)telicity.

4 What Are the Key Readings?

4.1 Salaberry and Shirai (2002)

This indispensable collection of studies provides both the beginner and the expert reader with a comprehensive and insightful retrospective look at the data, as well as presenting an attempt to reflect on the consistency of the various methodologies that brought about the different formulations of the LAH over the years. The volume also contains Andersen's 2002 paper. In his contribution, Andersen acknowledged that researchers engaged in research on the Tense-Aspect system needed a more rigorous research methodology that could include more dimensions of inquiry (e.g., event type, realis vs. irrealis distinction, etc.). He concluded that "the question we need to ask is: how does the learner discover the form to meaning relation encoded by the [past] marker when the learner first begins to productively use it in natural communication?" (p. 102). This more general question is still crucial today. It concerns the issue of the explanatory adequacy of the LAH. It can be rephrased very simply: in the acquisition of Aspect, what is the causal relationship between principles within the learner (either general or language-specific) and the regularities the learner finds in the input?

4.2 Zhao and Li (2009)

In addition to the classical Andersen and Shirai papers from the 1980s–1990s already quoted in this Element, I propose to the reader a more recent essay representing the most radical emergentist-connectionist perspective on the acquisition of Aspect. Because of its difficulty, this paper could not be commented upon in the previous, introductory sections, but it will attract the attention of the more informed (and skilled) reader. The study aims to demonstrate that an association between LAsp and GA can emerge from dynamic self-organization and Hebbian learning in connectionist networks (an automatic, computer-based device that weighs, records and compares the strength of association between cue and outcome based solely on the variable frequency of their co-occurrence), without the need of a priori assumptions about the structure of innate knowledge. The self-organizing maps (SOM) machine simulates a learner's exposure to the input and a learner's reaction (in terms of incremental automatic knowledge) to that exposure. The SOM machine requires no explicit teacher because learning is achieved solely by the system's organization in response to the input. The authors' point is that exposure to the input suffices for the learner to abstract away the category of, say, 'telic' and 'perfective'. There is no need to postulate that such categories are innate because they would 'emerge bottom-up' from the input.

References

Andersen, R. W. (1984). *Second language: A cross-linguistic perspective*, Rowley: Newbury House.

Andersen, R. W. (1993). Four operating principles and input distribution as explanations for underdeveloped and mature morphological systems. In K. Hyltenstam and Å. Viberg, eds., *Progression and regression in language: Sociocultural, neuropsychological and linguistic perspectives*, Cambridge: Cambridge University Press, pp. 309–339.

Andersen, R. W. (2002). The dimension of "Pastness." In R. Salaberry & Y. Shirai, Y. , eds., *The L2 acquisition of tense-aspect morphology*, Amsterdam and Philadelphia: John Benjamins, pp. 79–105.

Andersen, R. W. & Shirai, Y. (1994). Discourse motivations for some cognitive operating principles. *Studies in Second Language Acquisition*, 16(2), 133–156.

Andersen, R. W. & Shirai, Y. (1996). The primacy of aspect in first and second language acquisition: The pidgin/creole connection. In W. C. Ritchie & T. K. Bhatia, eds., *Handbook of second language acquisition*, New York: Academic Press, pp. 527–570.

Antinucci, F. & Miller, R. (1976). How children talk about what happened. *Journal of Child Language*, 3(2), 167–189.

Ayoun, D. & Rothman, J. (2013). Generative approaches to the L2 acquisition of temporal-aspectual-mood systems. In R. Salaberry & L. Comajoan, eds., *Research design and methodology in studies on L2 tense and aspect*, Boston: De Gruyter, pp. 119–156.

Baayen, R. H. (2010). Demythologizing the word frequency effect: A discriminative learning perspective. *The Mental Lexicon*, 5(3), 436–461.

Baggio, G., van Lambalgen, M. & Hagoort, P. (2008). Computing and recomputing discourse models: An ERP study. *Journal of Memory and Language*, 59(1), 36–53.

Bardovi-Harlig, K. (1992). The telling of a tale: Discourse structure and tense use in learner's narratives. In L. F. Bouton & Y. Kachru, eds., *Pragmatics and language learning*. Urbana-Champaign: Division of English as an International Language, University of Illinois, pp. 144–161.

Bardovi-Harlig, K. (1994). Anecdote or evidence? Evaluating support for hypotheses concerning the development of tense and aspect. In E. Tarone, S. M. Gass & A. D. Cohen, eds., *Research methodology in second language acquisition*. Hillsdale: Erlbaum, pp. 41–60.

Bardovi-Harlig, K. (1995). A narrative perspective on the development of the tense/aspect system in second language acquisition. *Studies in Second Language Acquisition*, 17, 263–291.

Bardovi-Harlig, K. (2000). *Tense and aspect in second language acquisition: Form, meaning, and use*. Oxford: Blackwell.

Bardovi-Harlig, K. (2002). Analyzing aspect. In R. Salaberry & Y. Shirai, eds., *The L2 acquisition of tense–aspect morphology*. Amsterdam/Philadelphia: John Benjamins, pp. 129–154.

Bardovi-Harlig, K. (2012). Second language acquisition. In R. Binnick, ed., *The Oxford handbook of tense and aspect*, Oxford: Oxford University Press. DOI: http://10.1093/oxfordhb/9780195381979.013.0016

Bardovi-Harlig, K. & Comajoan-Colomé, L. (2020). The aspect hypothesis and the acquisition of L2 past morphology in the last 20 years. A state-of-the-scholarship review. *Studies in Second Language Acquisition*, 1–31. DOI: https://doi.org/10.1017/S0272263120000194

Beckers, T., De Houwer, J. & Matute, H. (2007). Editorial: Human contingency learning. *The Quarterly Journal of Experimental Psychology*, 60(3), 289–290.

Bennett, M. & Partee, B. (2004). Towards the logic of tense and aspect in English. In B. Partee, ed., *Compositionality in Formal Semantics*. Oxford: Blackwell Publishing. https://doi.org/10.1002/9780470751305.ch4

Bertinetto, P. M. (1986). *Tempo, Aspetto e Azione nel verbo italiano: il sistema dell'indicativo (Tense, aspect and actionality in the Italian verb: The indicative system)*. Firenze: Accademia della Crusca.

Bertinetto, P. M. (2001). On a frequent misunderstanding in the temporal-aspectual domain: The "perfective-telic" confusion. In C. Cecchetto, G. Chierchia & M. T. Guasti, eds., *Semantic interfaces: Reference, anaphora, and aspect*, Stanford: CSLI Publications, pp. 177–210.

Bertinetto P. M & Delfitto D. (2000). Aspect vs actionality: Why they should be kept apart. In Ö. Dahl, ed., *Tense and aspect in the languages of Europe*, Berlin and New York: Mouton de Gruyter, pp. 189–225.

Bertinetto, P. M. & Noccetti, S. (2006). Prolegomena to ATAM acquisition. Theoretical premises and corpus labeling. *Quaderni del Laboratorio di Linguistica della SNS* (7): http://linguistica.sns.it/QLL/QLL06/Bertinetto_Noccetti.PDF

Binnick, R. (1991). *Time and the verb*. Oxford and New York: Oxford University Press.

Bley-Vroman, R. (1983) The comparative fallacy in interlanguage studies: The case of systematicity. *Language Learning*, 33(1), 1–17.

Bloom, L., Lifter, K. & Hafitz, J. (1980). Semantics of verbs and the development of verb inflection in child language. *Language*, 66(2), 386–412.

Borer, H. (2004). The grammar machine. In A. Alexiadou, E. Anagnostopoulou & M. Everaert, eds., *The unaccusativity puzzle*, Oxford: Oxford University Press, pp. 288–331.

Borik, O., González, P. & Verkuyl, H. (2003). Comparing tense systems: The primacy of the Pres/Past opposition. *Nordlyd*, 31(1), 13–29.

Botne, R. (2003). To die across languages: Toward a typology of achievement verbs. *Linguistic Typology* 7(2), 75–119.

Champollion, L. & Krifka, M. (2016). Mereology. In P. Dekker & M. Aloni, eds., *Cambridge handbook of formal semantics*. Cambridge: Cambridge University Press, pp. 513–541.

Chao, W. & Bach, E. (2009). On semantic universals and typology. In C. Collins, M. Christiansen & S. Edelman, eds., *Language Universals*. Oxford: Oxford University Press, pp. 152–173.

Comajoan, L. (2006). The aspect hypothesis: Development of morphology and appropriateness of use. *Language Learning*, 56(2), 201–268.

Comrie, B. (1976). *Aspect: An introduction to the study of verbal aspect and related problems*. Cambridge: Cambridge University Press.

Comrie, B. (1985). *Tense*. Cambridge: Cambridge University Press.

Cover, R. T. & Tonhauser, J. (2015). Theories of meaning in the field: Temporal and aspectual reference. In R. Bochnak & L. Matthewson, eds., *Methodologies in Semantic Fieldwork*. Oxford: Oxford University Press, pp. 306–350.

Cruse, A. (1997). *Lexical semantics*. Oxford: Oxford University Press.

Dahl, Ö. (1985). *Tense and aspect systems*. Oxford: Blackwell.

Depraetere, I. (1995). On the necessity of distinguishing between (un)boundedness and (a)telicity. *Linguistics and Philosophy* 18(1), 1–19.

De Swart, H. (1998). Aspect shift and coercion. *Natural Language and Linguistic Theory* 16, 347–385.

Diaubalik, T. & Guijarro-Fuentes, P. (2019). The strength of L1 effects on tense and aspect: How German learners of L2 Spanish deal with acquisitional problems. *Language acquisition*, 26(3), 282–301. DOI: http://10.1080/10489223.2018.1554663.

Díaz, L., Bel, A. & Bekiou, K. (2007). Interpretable and uninterpretable features in the acquisition of Spanish past tenses. In J. Liceras, H. Zobl & H. Goodluck, eds., *The role of formal features in second language acquisition*. Mhawah: Lawrence Erlbaum, pp. 485–511.

Dietrich, R., Klein, W. & Noyau, C. (1995). *The acquisition of temporality in a second language*. Amsterdam: John Benjamins.

Di Sciullo, A. M. & Slabakova, R. (2005). Quantification and aspect. In H. Verkuyl, H. De Swart & A. van Hout, eds., *Perspectives on aspect*. Dordrecht: Springer, pp. 61–80.

Dowty, D. R. (1979). *Word meaning and Montague grammar*. Dordrecht: Reidel.

Dowty, D. (1991). Thematic proto-roles and argument selection. *Language*, 67(3), 547–619.

Dryer, M. & Haspelmath, M. (eds.). (2013). *The world atlas of language structures online*. Leipzig: Max Planck Institute for Evolutionary Anthropology, http://wals.info

Ebert, K. (1995). Ambiguous perfect-progressive forms across languages. In P. M. Bertinetto, V. Bianchi, Ö. Dahl & M. Squartini, eds., *Temporal reference, aspect and actionality*, vol. 2. Torino: Rosenberg & Sellier, pp. 185–204.

Ellis, N. C. (2016). Cognition, corpora, and computing: Triangulating research in usage-based language learning. *Language Learning*, 67(51), 40–65. DOI: https://doi.org/10.1111/lang.12215

Ellis, N. C. & Ferreira-Junior F. G. (2009). Construction learning as a function of frequency, frequency distribution, and function. *The Modern Language Journal*, 93(3), 370–385.

Filip, H. (2004). The telicity parameter revisited. In R. Young, ed., *Semantics and linguistic theory (SALT) XIV*. Ithaca: CLC Publications. Department of Linguistics, Cornell University, pp 92–109.

Filip, H. (2011). Aspectual class and Aktionsart. In C. Maienborn, K. von Heusinger & P. Portner, eds., *Semantics: An international handbook of natural language meaning*, vol. 1. Berlin/New York: De Gruyter Mouton, pp. 1186–1217.

Filip, H. (2012). Lexical aspect. In R. Binnik, ed., *The Oxford handbook of tense and aspect*. Oxford: Oxford University Press, pp. 721–751.

Foley, W. A. & Van Valin, R. D. (1984). *Functional syntax and universal grammar*. Cambridge: Cambridge University Press.

Gabriele, A., Martohardjono, G. & McClure, W. (2003). Why swimming is just as difficult as dying for Japanese learners of English. *ZAS Papers in Linguistics*, 29, 85–103.

Gabriele, A. & McClure, W. (2011). Why some imperfectives are interpreted imperfectly: A study of Chinese learners of Japanese. *Language Acquisition*, 18(1), 39–83.

Garey, H. B. (1957). Verbal aspects in French. *Language*, 33(2), 91–110.

Gass, S., Behney, J. & Plonsky, L. (2013). *Second language acquisition. An introductory course*. New York/London: Routledge.

Giacalone Ramat, A. (1995). Tense and aspect in learner Italian. In P. M. Bertinetto, V. Bianchi, O. Dahl & M. Squartini, eds., *Temporal reference, aspect and actionality*, vol. 2. Torino: Rosenberg & Sellier, pp. 289–307.

Giacalone Ramat, A. & Rastelli S. (2013). The qualitative analysis of actionality in learner language. In R. Salaberry and L. Comajoan, eds., *Research design and methodology in studies on L2 tense and aspect*. Amsterdam/ Philadelphia: Walter de Gruyter, pp. 391–422.

Giorgi, A. & Pianesi, F. (1997). *Tense and aspect: From semantics to morpho-syntax*. Oxford/New York: Oxford University Press.

Goldberg, A. (2006). *Constructions at work: The nature of generalization in language*. Oxford: Oxford University Press

González, P. (2013). Research design. A two-way predicational system is better than a four-way approach. In R. Salaberry & Y. Shirai, eds., *The L2 acquisition of tense–aspect morphology*. Amsterdam/Philadelphia: John Benjamins, pp. 159–186

González, P. & Quintana-Hernández, L. (2018). Inherent aspect and L1 transfer in the L2 acquisition of Spanish grammatical aspect. *Modern Language Journal*, 102(3), 611–625. DOI: 10.1111/modl.12502

Gries, S. T. (2018). Mechanistic formal approaches to language acquisition. Yes, but at the right level(s) of resolution. *Linguistic Approaches to Bilingualism*, 8(6), 733–737.

Gries, S. & Stefanowitsch, A. (2004). Extending collostructional analysis: A corpus-based perspective on "alternations". *International Journal of Corpus Linguistics*, 9(1), 97–129. https://doi.org/10.1075/ijcl.9.1.06gri

Gvozdanović, J. (2012). Perfective and imperfective aspect. In R. Binnick, ed., *The Oxford handbook of tense and aspect*, Oxford: Oxford University Press. DOI: http://10.1093/oxfordhb/9780195381979.013.0027

Haspelmath, M. (2001). The European linguistic area: Standard Average European. In M. Haspelmath, E. König, W. Oesterreicher & W. Raible, eds., *Language typology and language universals*. Berlin/New York: De Gruyter, pp. 1492–1510.

Hopper, P. J. (1979). Aspect and foregrounding in discourse. In T. Givón, ed., *Syntax and semantics: Discourse and syntax*. New York: Academic Press, pp. 213–241.

Housen, A. (2000). Verb semantics and the acquisition of tense-aspect in L2 English. *Studia Linguistica*, 54(2), 249–259. https://doi.org/10.1111/1467-9582.00064

Housen, A. (2002).The development of tense–aspect in English as a second language and the variable influence of inherent aspect. In R. Salaberry & Y. Shirai, eds., *The L2 acquisition of tense–aspect morphology*. Amsterdam and Philadelphia: John Benjamins, pp. 155–197.

Huang, P. Y. (2008). The Aspect Hypothesis and L2 learners' awareness of lexical aspect. Poster presented in *The acquisition of tense, aspect and mood in L1 and L2* Conference. Birmingham: Aston University.

Izquierdo, J. & Collins, L. (2008). The facilitative role of L1 influence in tense–aspect marking: A comparison of hispanophone and anglophone learners of French. *Modern Language Journal*, 92(3), 350–368.

Jackendoff, R. (1997). *The architecture of the language faculty.* Cambridge: Cambridge University Press.

Kamp, H. & Rohrer, C. (1983). Tense in text. In A. von Stechow, ed., *Meaning, use and interpretation of language.* Berlin/New York: Mouton – De Gruyter, pp. 250–269.

Kazanina, N. & Phillips, C. (2003). Temporal reference frames and the imperfective paradox. In G. Garding & M. Tsujimura, eds., *Proceedings of WCCFL 22.* Somerville: Cascadilla Press, pp. 287–300.

Kazanina, N. & Phillips, C. (2007). A developmental perspective on the imperfective paradox. *Cognition*, 105(1), pp. 65–102.

Kenny, A. (1963). *Action, emotion and will.* London: Routledge.

Klein, W. (1994). *Time in language.* London: Routledge.

Klein, W., Li, P. & Hendriks, H. (2000). Aspect and assertion in Mandarin Chinese. *Natural Language and Linguistic Theory*, 18, 723–770. http://doi18.723-770.10.1023/A:1006411825993

Krifka, M. (1992). A compositional semantics for multiple focus constructions. *Proceedings of Semantics and Linguistic Theory (SALT) 1.* Cornell Working Papers in Linguistics, 10, 127–158.

Krifka, M. (1998). The origins of telicity. In S. Rothstein, ed., *Events and grammar.* Dordrecht: Kluwer, pp. 197–235.

Labeau, E. (2005). *Beyond the aspect hypothesis. Tense–aspect development in advanced L2 French.* Oxford/Bern: Peter Lang.

Lakshmanan U. & Selinker, L. (2001). Analysing interlanguage: How do we know what learners know? *Second Language Research*, 17, 393–420.

Landman, F. (1992). The progressive. *Natural Language Semantics*, 1(1), 1–32.

Lardiere, D. (2003). The comparative fallacy revisited: A reply to Lakshmanan and Selinker (2001). *Second Language Research*, 19, 129–143.

Lee, E. H. & Kim, H. Y. (2007). On cross-linguistic variations in imperfective aspect: The case of L2 Korean. *Language Learning*, 57(4), 651–685. DOI: 10.1111/j.1467-9922.2007.00431.x

Lenci, A. & Zarcone, A. (2009). Un modello stocastico della classificazione azionale. (A stocastic model of actional classification) In G. Ferrari, R. Benatti & M. Mosca, eds., *Atti del XL congresso internazionale della Società di Linguistica Italiana.* Roma: Bulzoni, pp. 125–148.

Levin, B. & Rappoport Hovav, M. (1995). *Unaccusativity.* Cambridge: MIT Press.

Li, C. & Thompson, S. (1981). *Mandarin Chinese: A functional reference grammar*. Berkeley: University of California Press.

Li, P. (2000). The acquisition of lexical and grammatical aspect in a self-organizing feature-map model. In L. Gleitman & J. Aravind, eds., *Proceedings of the 22nd annual conference of the Cognitive Science Society*. Hillsdale: Erlbaum, pp. 304–309.

Li, P. (2002). Emergent semantic structure and language acquisition: A dynamic perspective. In C.-K. Leong, G. Ding-Guo & H. Kao, eds., *Cognitive neuroscience studies of the Chinese language*. Hong Kong: The Hong Kong University Press, pp. 79–98.

Li, P. & Bowerman, M. (1998). The acquisition of lexical and grammatical aspect in Chinese. *First Language*, 18(54), 311–350. DOI: 10.1177/014272379801805404

Li, P. & Shirai, Y. (2000). *The acquisition of lexical and grammatical aspect*. Berlin: Mouton De Gruyter.

Malaia, E., Wilbur, R. B. & Weber-Fox, C. (2009). ERP evidence for telicity effects on syntactic processing in garden-path sentences. *Brain and Language*, 108(3), 145–158.

Matthews, S. & Yip, V. (2013). *Cantonese: A comprehensive grammar*. London: Routledge.

McClure, W. (2003). Change of state syntax. Unpublished paper. New York: The Queens College and Graduate Center, CUNY.

McManus, K. (2013). Prototypical influence in second language acquisition: What now for the Aspect Hypothesis. *IRAL*, 51(3), 299–322.

McManus, K. (2015). L1–L2 differences in the acquisition of form–meaning pairings: A comparison of English and German learners of French. *Canadian Modern Language Review*, 71(2), 155–181.

Michaelis, L. A. (2004). Type shifting in cosntruction grammar: An integrated approach to aspectual cohercion. *Cognitive Linguistics*. DOI: http://10.1515/cogl.2004.001

Mlynarczyk, A. K. (2004). *Aspectual Pairing in Polish*. PhD dissertation. Utrecht: Utrecht University Repository.

Moens, M. & Steedman, M. (2005). Temporal ontology and temporal reference. In I. Mani, J. Pusteiovskj & R. Gaizauskas, eds., *The language of time: A reader*. Oxford: Oxford University Press, pp. 93–114.

Montrul, S. (2002). Incomplete acquisition and attrition of Spanish tense/aspect distinctions in adult bilinguals. *Bilingualism: Language and Cognition*, 5(1), 39–68.

Montrul, S. (2009) Knowledge of tense-aspect and mood in Spanish heritage speakers. *International Journal of Bilingualism*, 13(2), 239–269.

Montrul, S. & Perpiñán, S. (2011). Assessing differences and similarities between instructed heritage language learners and L2 learners in their knowledge of Spanish tense-aspect and mood (TAM) morphology. *Heritage Language Journal*, 8(1), 90–133.

Montrul, S. & Slabakova, R. (2003). Competence similarities between native and near-native speakers: An investigation of the preterite-imperfect contrast in Spanish. *Studies in Second Language Acquisition*, 25(3), 351–398.

Morgan-Short, K. & Ullman M.T. (2011). The neurocognition of second language. In A. Mackey & S. Gass, eds., *The Routledge handbook of second language acquisition*. London: Routledge, pp. 282–299.

Mueller, C. M. (2018). Initial acquisition of tense aspect morphology in an artificial language. *Second Language Research*. DOI: http://10.1177/0267658317750219

Nossalik, L. (2007). Slavic perfective prefixes: Are they telicity markers? In M. Radišić, ed., *Proceedings of the 2007 Annual Conference of the Canadian Linguistic Association*, http://homes.chass.utoronto.ca/~cla-acl/actes2007/Nossalik.pdf

Osterhout, L., McLaughlin, J., Pitkänen, I., Frenck-Mestre, C. & Molinaro, N. (2006). Novice learners, longitudinal designs and event-related potentials: A means for exploring the neurocognition of second language processing. In P. Indefrey & M. Gullberg, eds., *The cognitive neuroscience of second language acquisition*. Malden/Oxford: Blackwell, pp. 199–230.

Pace, A., Levine, D. F., Golinkoff, R. M., Carver, L. J. & Hirsh-Pasek, K. (2020). Keeping the end in mind: Preliminary brain and behavioral evidence for broad attention to endpoints in pre-linguistic infants. *Infant Behavior and Development*. DOI:http://10.1016/j.infbeh.2020.101425

Parsons, T. (1989). The progressive in English: Events, states and processes. *Linguistics and Philosophy*, 12, 213–241.

Pustejovsky, J. (1991). The syntax of event structure. *Cognition*, 41(1), 47–81. DOI: http://10.1016/0010-0277(91)90032-Y

Rastelli, S. (2008). A compositional account of L2 verb actionality and the aspect hypothesis. *Lingue e Linguaggio*, 7(2), 261–289.

Rastelli, S. (2009). Lexical aspect too is learned: Data from Italian learner corpora. In A. Saxena & A. Viberg, eds., *Multilingualism*. Uppsala: Edita Astra Varos, pp. 272–282.

Rastelli, S. (2019). The imperfective paradox in a second language: A dynamic completion-entailment test. *Lingua*. 231, 102709. DOI: http://10.1016/j.lingua.2019.06.0100024–3841

Rastelli, S. (2020). Contingency learning and the emergence of the perfective in L2 Italian: a study on lexeme–morpheme associations with ΔP.

Corpus Linguistics and Linguistic Theory. https://doi.org/10.1515/cllt-2019–0071

Rastelli, S. & Vernice, M. (2013). Developing actional competence and the building blocks of telicity in L2 Italian. *IRAL – International Review of Applied Linguistics in Language Teaching*, 51(1), 55–75.

Reeder, P. A., Newport, E. L. & Aslin, R. N. (2010). Novel words in novel contexts: The role of distributional information in form-class category learning. In S. Ohlsson & R. Catrambone, eds., *Proceedings of the 32nd Annual Meeting of the Cognitive Science Society*. Austin: Cognitive Science Society, pp. 2063–2068.

Reichenbach, H. (1947). *Elements of symbolic logic*. Free Press, New York.

Roberts, L. & Liszka, S.A. (2013). Processing tense/aspect agreement violations online in the second language: A self-paced reading study with French and German L2 learners of English. *Second Language Research*, 29(4) 413–439.

Roberts, L. & Liszka, S.A. (2019). Grammatical aspect and L2 learners' online processing of temporarily ambiguous sentences in English: A self-paced reading study with German, Dutch and French L2 learners. *Second Language Research*. DOI: http://10.1177/0267658319895551.

Rohde, A. (2002). The aspect hypothesis in naturalistic L2 acquisition: What uninflected and non-target-like verb forms in early interlanguage tells us. In R. Salaberry & Y. Shirai, eds., *The L2 acquisition of tense-aspect morphology*. Amsterdam/Philadelphia: John Benjamins, pp. 199–220.

Romagno, D., Rota, G., Ricciardi, E. & Pietrini, P. (2012). Where the brain appreciates the final state of an event: The neural correlates of telicity, 123(1), 68–74. *Brain and Language* http://dx.doi.org/10.1016/j.bandl.2012.06.003

Rosch, E, (1975) Cognitive representations of semantic categories. *Journal of Experimental Psychology*, 104(3), 192–233.

Ryle, G. (1949). *The concept of mind*. London: Barnes and Noble.

Ryu, J.-Y., Horie, K. & Shirai, Y. (2015). Acquisition of the Korean imperfective aspect markers –ko iss– and –a iss– by Japanese learners: A multiple-factor account. *Language Learning*, 65(4), 791–823.

Salaberry, M. R. (2008). *Marking past tense in second language acquisition: A theoretical model*. London: Continuum Press.

Salaberry M. R. (2011) Assessing the effect of lexical aspect and grounding on the acquisition of L2 Spanish past tense morphology among L1 English speakers. *Bilingualism: Language and Cognition*, 14 (2), 184–202.

Salaberry, M. R., Comajoan, L. & González, P. (2013). Integrating the analyses of tense and aspect across research and methodological frameworks. In R. Salaberry & L. Comajoan, eds., *Research design and methodology in studies on L2 tense and aspect*. Boston/Berlin: De Gruyter, pp. 423–450.

Salaberry M. R. & Martins, C. (2014). Cross-linguistic transfer of core aspectual conceptualizations in Portuguese and Spanish Theoretical and methodological factors. In P. Amaral & A. M. Carvalho, eds., *Portuguese-Spanish interfaces: Diachrony, synchrony, and contact.* Amsterdam/Philadelphia: John Benjamins Publishing, pp. 335–355.

Salaberry, R. & Shirai, Y. (2002) (eds.). The L2 acquisition of tense-aspect morphology. Amsterdam/Philadelphia: John Benjamins Publishing.

Shirai, Y. (2002). The prototype hypothesis of tense-aspect acquisition in second language. In R. Salaberry & Y. Shirai, eds., The L2 acquisition of tense-aspect morphology. Amsterdam/Philadelphia: John Benjamins Publishing, pp. 455–478.

Shirai, Y. (2007). The aspect hypothesis, the comparative fallacy, and the validity of obligatory context analysis: A reply to Lardiere (2003). *Second Language Research*, 23, 51–64.

Shirai, Y. (2013). Defining and coding data: Lexical aspect in L2 studies. In R. Salaberry & L. Comajoan, eds., *Research design and methodology in studies on L2 tense and aspect.* Boston/Berlin: De Gruyter, pp. 271–308.

Shirai, Y. (2016). The current state of the Aspect Hypothesis: Exceptions that prove the rule. Plenary presentation at Tense Aspect Mood in Second Languages (TAML2) VII. University of York, June 16, 2016.

Shirai, Y. & Andersen, R. W. (1995). The acquisition of tense-aspect morphology: A prototype account. *Language* 71(4), 743–762.

Slabakova, R. (2000). L1 transfer revisited: The L2 acquisition of telicity marking in English by Spanish and Bulgarian native speakers. *Linguistics*, 38(368), DOI: http://10.1515/ling.2000.004

Slabakova, R. (2001). *Telicity in the second language.* Amsterdam/Philadelphia: John Benjamins Publishing.

Slabakova, R. (2006). Is there a critical period for semantics? *Second Language Research*, 22(3), 302–338.

Slabakova, R. & Montrul, S. (2000). Acquiring semantic-properties of preterite and imperfect tenses in L2 Spanish. In S. C. Howell, S. A. Fish & T. Keith-Lucas, eds., *Proceedings of the 24th Boston University Conference on Language Development.* Somerville: Cascadilla Press, pp. 534–545.

Slabakova, R. & Montrul, S. (2002). On viewpoint aspect interpretation and its L2 acquisition: A UG perspective. In R. Salaberry and Y. Shirai, eds., *The L2 acquisition of tense–aspect morphology.* Amsterdam/Philadelphia: John Benjamins, pp. 363–395.

Slabakova, R. & Montrul, S. (2007). L2 acquisition at the grammar–discourse interface: Aspectual shifts in L2 Spanish. In J. Liceras, H. Zobl &

H. Goodluck, eds., *Formal features in second language acquisition.* Mahwah: Lawrence Erlbaum Associates, pp. 452–483.

Slobin, D. (1979). *Psycholinguistics.* Glenview: Scott, Foresman and Company.

Smith, C. (1991). *The parameter of aspect.* Dordrecht: Springer.

Smollet, R. (2005). Quantized direct objects don't delimit after all. In H. Verkuyl, H. de Swart & A. van Hout, eds., *Perspectives on Aspect.* Springer: Dordrecht, pp. 41–60.

Sorace, A. (2004). Gradience at the lexico–syntax interface: Evidence from auxiliary selection and implications for unaccusativity. In A. Alexiadou, E. Anagnostopoulou & M. Everaert, eds., *The unaccusativity puzzle.* Oxford/New York: Oxford University Press, pp. 243–268.

Tatevosov, S. (2002). The parameter of actionality. *Linguistic Typology*, 6(3), 317–401.

Taylor, J. R. (1989). *Linguistic categorization: Prototypes in linguistic theory.* Oxford: Oxford University Press.

Tong, X. & Shirai, Y. (2016). L2 acquisition of Mandarin zai and –le. *Chinese as Second Language Acquisition Research (CASLAR)*, 5(1), 1–26.

Tracy-Ventura, N. & Cuesta Medina, J. A. (2018). Can native-speaker corpora help explain L2 acquisition of tense and aspect? A study of the "input". *International Journal of Learner Corpus Research*, 4(2), 277–300.

Travis, deMena L. (1994). Event Phrase and a theory of functional categories. In P. Koskinen, ed., *Proceedings of the 1994 Canadian Linguistic Association meeting at the University of Calgary.* Toronto: Working Papers in Linguistics, pp. 559–570.

Travis, deMena L. (2010). *Inner aspect: The articulation of VP.* Dordrecht: Springer.

van Hout, A. (2004). Unaccusativity as telicity checking. In A. Alexiadou, E. Anagnostopoulou & Martin Everaert, eds., *The unaccusativity puzzle.* Oxford: Oxford University Press, pp. 60–83.

van Hout, A. (2008a). Acquiring telicity crosslinguistically: On the acquisition of telicity entailments associated with transitivity. In M. Bowermann & P. Brown, eds., *Crosslinguistic perspectives on argument structure.* New York/London: Lawrence Erlbaum Associates, pp. 255–278.

Van Hout, A. (2008b). Acquiring perfectivity and telicity in Dutch, Italian and Polish. *Lingua*, 118(11), 1740–1765.

van Hout, A., de Swart, H. & Verkuyl, H. (2005). Introducing perspectives on aspect. In H. Verkuyl, H. de Swart & A. van Hout, eds., *Perspectives on aspect.* Springer: Dordrecht, pp. 1–19.

VanPatten, B., Keating, G. & Leeser, M. (2012). Missing verbal inflections as a representational problem: Evidence from on-line methodology. *Linguistic Approaches to Bilingualism*, 2(2), 109–140.

van Valin, R. D. (1990). Semantic parameters of split intransitivity. *Language*, 66(2), 221–260.

van Valin, R. D (2005). *Exploring the syntax–semantics interface*. Cambridge: Cambridge University Press.

Vendler, Z. (1957). Verbs and times. *Philosophical Review*, 56(2), 143–160. Reprinted in Z. Vendler (1967). *Linguistics in Philosophy*. Ithaca: Cornell University.

Verkuyl, H. J. (1993). *A theory of aspectuality*. Cambridge: Cambridge University Press.

Verkuyl, H. J. (1999). *Aspectual issues: Studies on time and quantity*. Stanford: CSLI Publications.

Verkuyl, H. J. (2005). Aspectual composition: surveying the ingredients. In H. J. Verkuyl, H. de Swart & A. van Hout, eds, *Perspectives on aspect*. Dordrecht: Springer, pp. 19–39.

Verkuyl, H. (2015). *Aspectual composition and aspectual classes: What did Aristotle really say to Ryle, Kenny and Vendler*? Unpublished article, UIL OTS, Utrecht University.

Viberg, Å. (2002). Basic verbs in lexical progression and regression. In P. Burmeister, T. Piske & Andreas Rohde, eds., *An integrated view of language development: Papers in honor of Henning Wode*. Wissenschaftlicher: Verlag Trier, pp. 109–134.

Vikner, C. & Vikner, S. (1997). The aspectual complexity of the simple past in English. A comparison with French and Danish. In C. Bache & A. Klinge, eds., *Sounds, structures and senses: Essays presented to Niels Davidsen-Nielsen on the occasion of his sixtieth birthday*. Odense: Odense University Press, pp. 267–284.

Vogel, E. K. (2017). *Native vs. non-native processing of Spanish: The role of lexical and grammatical aspect*. Unpublished PhD Thesis, retrieved from http://purl.flvc.org/fsu/fd/FSU_2017SP_Vogel_fsu_0071E_13727

von Stutterheim, C. & Klein, W. (1989). Referential movement in descriptive and narrative discourse. In R. Dietrich & C. F. Graumann, eds., *Language processing in social context*. Amsterdam: Elsevier, pp. 39–76.

Wagner, L. (2001). Aspectual influences on early tense comprehension. *Journal of Child Language*, 28(3), 661–681.

Wagner, L. (2002). Understanding completion entailment in the absence of agency cues. *Journal of Child Language*, 29(1), 109–125.

Weist, R. (2002). The first language acquisition of tense and aspect: A review. In R. Salaberry and Y. Shirai, eds., *The L2 acquisition of tense–aspect morphology.* Amsterdam/Philadelphia: John Benjamins, pp. 21–78.

Weist, R., Wysocka, H., Witkowska-Stadnik, K., Buczowska, E. & Konieczna, E. (1984). The defective tense hypothesis: On the emergence of tense and aspect in child Polish. *Journal of Child Language*, 11(2), 347–374.

Wulff, S., Ellis, N., Bardovi-Harlig, K., Leblanc, C. J. & Römer, U. (2009). The acquisition of tense-aspect: Converging evidence from corpora and telicity ratings. *The Modern Language Journal*, 93(3), 354–369. doi:10.1111/j.1540-4781.2009.00895.x

Zhao, X. & Li, P. (2009). Acquisition of aspect in self-organizing connectionist models. *Linguistics* 47(5), 1075–1112.

Acknowledgements

I would like to thank the series editor and the editorial staff at CUP for caring so much about the publication of this book. I am also grateful to the reviewers for their insightful comments on an early version of the manuscript.

Cambridge Elements

Second Language Acquisition

Alessandro Benati
The University of Hong Kong
Alessandro Benati is Director of CAES at The University of Hong Kong (HKU). He is known for his work in second language acquisition and second language teaching. He has published ground-breaking research on the pedagogical framework called Processing Instruction. He is co-editor of a new online series for Cambridge University Press, a member of the REF Panel 2021, and Honorary Professor at York St John University.

John W. Schwieter
Wilfrid Laurier University, Ontario
John W. Schwieter is Associate Professor of Spanish and Linguistics, and Faculty of Arts Teaching Scholar, at Wilfrid Laurier University. His research interests include psycholinguistic and neurolinguistic approaches to multilingualism and language acquisition; second language teaching and learning; translation and cognition; and language, culture, and society.

About the Series

Second Language Acquisition showcases a high-quality set of updatable, concise works that address how learners come to internalize the linguistic system of another language and how they make use of that linguistic system. Contributions reflect the interdisciplinary nature of the field, drawing on theories, hypotheses, and frameworks from education, linguistics, psychology, and neurology, among other disciplines. Each Element in this series addresses several important questions: What are the key concepts?; What are the main branches of research?; What are the implications for SLA?; What are the implications for pedagogy?; What are the new avenues for research?; and What are the key readings?

Cambridge Elements

Second Language Acquisition

Elements in the Series

Proficiency Predictors in Sequential Bilinguals
Lynette Austin, Arturo E. Hernandez and John W. Schwieter

Implicit Language Aptitude
Gisela Granena

Generative Second Language Acquisition
Roumyana Slabakova, Tania Leal, Amber Dudley and Micah Stack

The Acquisition of Aspect in a Second Language
Stefano Rastelli

A full series listing is available at www.cambridge.org/esla

Printed in the United States
By Bookmasters